D0576272

# EYEWITNESS
# TO DISASTER

# EYEWITNESS TO DISASTER

## DAN PERKES

GALLERY BOOKS
An Imprint of W. H. Smith Publishers Inc.
112 Madison Avenue
New York City 10016

150904

© Copyright 1985 by Hammond Incorporated
All rights reserved. No part of this book may be reproduced
or transmitted in any form or by any means, electronic or
mechanical, including photocopying, recording, or by any information retrieval system, without permission in writing
from the Publisher.

Prepared and produced by Wieser & Wieser, Inc.
80 Madison Avenue, Penthouse B
New York, New York 10016

Published by Gallery Books, an imprint of W. H. Smith
Publishers Inc.
112 Madison Avenue
New York, New York 10016

Book design by Melcon Tashian

Maps prepared by Hammond Incorporated

All photos in this publication, unless otherwise specified,
have been supplied by The Associated Press.

Photo that accompanies poem page 8 shows victims of the
*General Slocum* marine disaster of 1904.

**Library of Congress Cataloging in Publication Data**

Perkes, Dan.
    Eyewitness to disaster.

    Includes index.
    1. Disasters.  I. Title.
D445.P39   1985         904         85-3151
ISBN 0-8317-3093-5

Printed in Hong Kong

R
904
P447e

To Norma.
And to all those whose original
accounts and photographs
made this volume possible.

# CONTENTS

**AND ONLY ONE RETURNED**
*Monongah Coal Mine Explosion* / WEST VIRGINIA 1907 **16**

**HELL'S HUNDRED ACRES**
*Triangle Shirtwaist Co. Fire* / NEW YORK 1911 **24**

**DEATH TAKES AN OUTING**
Eastland *Ship Disaster* / CHICAGO 1915 **30**

**HOLOCAUST ON THE HIGH SEAS**
*Burning of the* Morro Castle / OFF NEW JERSEY 1934 **38**

**IT TOOK ONLY A SPARK**
*School Explosion* / NEW LONDON, TEXAS 1937 **48**

**THE END OF AN ERA**
Hindenburg *Explosion* / LAKEHURST, NEW JERSEY 1937 **56**

**A NIGHT TO FORGET**
*Cocoanut Grove Night Club Fire* / BOSTON 1942 **66**

**A DAY AT THE CIRCUS**
*"Big Top" Circus Fire* / HARTFORD 1944 **74**

**FROM OUT OF THE FOG**
*Bomber Crash into Empire State Building* /
NEW YORK 1945 **82**

**DEATH—THE UNINVITED GUEST**
*Winecoff Hotel Fire* / ATLANTA 1946 **88**

**A CARGO OF DOOM**
Grandcamp *Ship Explosion* / TEXAS CITY, TEXAS 1947 **96**

**PRIDE OF THE GREAT LAKES**
Noronic *Burns at Pier* / TORONTO 1949 **104**

**UNSCHEDULED STOP AT RICHMOND HILL**
*Commuter Train Wreck* / LONG ISLAND 1950 **110**

**LEGEND OF THE HUACOS**
*Southwest Tornado* / WACO, TEXAS 1953 **118**

**COLLISION AT SEA**
*Sinking of the* Andrea Doria /. OFF NANTUCKET 1956 **124**

**A CHRISTMAS REUNION**
*Mid-air Plane Collision* / NEW YORK 1956
**132**

**IT'S HOW YOU PLAY THE GAME**
*Soccer Riot* / LIMA, PERU 1964
**142**

**DEATH OF A GENERATION**
*Coal Slag Slide* / ABERFAN, WALES 1966
**148**

**CAMILLE WAS NO LADY**
*Hurricane Camille* / U.S. GULF COAST 1969
**154**

**A KILLING WINTER**
*Avalanches* / VAL D'ISÈRE AND PLATEAU D'ASSY,
FRANCE 1970
**160**

**THE DAY THE MOUNTAIN FELL**
*Earthquake and Landslides* / PERU 1970
**166**

**FAMINE IN THE SUB-SAHARA**
*Drought-Caused Famine* / AFRICA 1973–1975
**172**

**THE "TOWERING INFERNO"—
BRAZIL STYLE**
*Skyscraper Fire* / SÃO PAULO 1974
**178**

**THE NIGHT THE EARTH DANCED**
*Central American Earthquake* / GUATEMALA 1976
**184**

**LAST VACATION IN SPAIN**
*Tank Truck Explosion* / TARRAGONA, SPAIN 1978
**190**

**DAY OF THE VOLCANO**
*Volcano Eruption* / MOUNT ST. HELENS,
WASHINGTON 1980
**196**

**DANCE OF DEATH**
*Hotel Walkway Collapse* / KANSAS CITY 1981
**206**

**APPENDIX: MAJOR DISASTERS
SINCE 1900**
**212**

**INDEX**
**223**

There is a Reaper, whose name is Death,
      And, with his sickle keen,
He reaps the bearded grain at a breath,
      And the flowers that grow between.
—HENRY WADSWORTH LONGFELLOW
"The Reaper and the Flowers"

This is a book about tragedy. Of stark, human tragedy. Of many tragedies. It is about disasters—those catastrophic events which overwhelm, which kill, which maim. Even more so, it is a chronicle of humanity's inability to control some of these events—be they natural or created by mankind's own shortcomings. Once such wrathful forces are unleashed, man cannot change the outcome.

Not when Mount Vesuvius erupted in A.D. 79, destroying the cities of Pompeii and Herculaneum, bringing death to thousands of their citizens.

Not in the 1340s when bubonic plague, the Black Death, swept across Europe and Asia and was said to have killed 25 million men, women and children.

Not even when yellow fever raged through Philadelphia in the late 18th century and claimed thousands of lives. Or in 1902 when volcanic Mount Pelée erupted on the island of Martinique in the French West Indies and killed all but two of the 30,000 residents of St-Pierre.

Nature brought havoc to a large, modern American city for the first time in the San Francisco earthquake. The nightmare for California's "Golden Gate" city began at 5:15 on the morning of April 18, 1906. The earth above the San Andreas fault writhed and heaved under a force greater than all the explosives used in World War II. For three days, San Francisco burned in an inferno that consumed five square miles of city, from the Nob Hill mansions of the rich to the sleazy whorehouses of the Barbary Coast. By the time it was over, nearly 700 had perished, another 250,000 were homeless and damage was counted at more than half a billion dollars. As the picture on the previous pages testifies. the destruction was almost total.

The San Francisco earthquake was a natural disaster, a manifestation of forces outside human control. In this 20th century we have seen other,

even greater, manifestations of nature on the rampage.

One such was the disastrous hurricane which blasted Galveston Island on the Texas Gulf Coast in 1900 and killed about 6,000 people in one of the worst tragedies ever recorded in North America.

Or the great Japanese earthquake which virtually destroyed the cities of Tokyo and Yokohama in 1923, taking more than 100,000 lives.

And the great dust storms which rolled over much of the Midwest and Southwest United States during the 1930s, ravaging once-fertile farmlands as well as the hopes and dreams of countless tens of thousands of those who dwelt on those lands.

Then there have been other disastrous events in which man, himself, was to blame because of shortsightedness, ineptitude, or varying degrees of both.

On June 15, 1904, for example, the steamer *General Slocum* moved down the East River in New York City, carrying some 2,000 people on an excursion sponsored by St. Mark's German Lutheran Church. More than 1,000—mostly women and children—never returned home. The steamer caught fire, and the victims either drowned or died by fire—within 300 feet of the shoreline. The high toll was laid to the actions of the vessel's captain, who panicked and did not quickly make for shore after the fire started.

April 15, 1912, is the date of one of the most infamous disasters in history. The White Star liner *Titanic*, an "unsinkable" ship, struck an iceberg in the North Atlantic and sank with a loss of more than 1,500 lives. The overconfident captain and senior officers had failed to heed iceberg warnings. And the line had failed to provide enough lifeboats.

But the lessons of the *Titanic* hadn't been learned when, sixteen years later, the old British steamship *Vestris* left Hoboken, New Jersey, with a slight port list and a 200-ton overload. She foundered and sank in a nor'easter the next day, taking 110 people—mostly passengers—down with her.

In compiling this volume, the author literally had a mountain of resource material from which to choose because disasters occur worldwide with disturbing frequency. For example, the account of the earthquake in Guatemala was written as dispatches and photos arrived from the scene of the devastation. And even as this book was in its final editing, India was mourning the deaths of more than 2,000 men, women and children from toxic gas that leaked from a Union Carbide chemical plant at Bhopal, India.

In making the final selection of disasters, it was decided to concentrate on those events—some monumental and some little remembered—which had the benefit of broad coverage both in words and pictures at the time those events occurred.

# AND ONLY ONE RETURNED

**T**he entrance to Monongah No. 6 is lined with horrified spectators to the worst mining tragedy in United States history. Others stand on the stark bank above, waiting to learn the extent of the tragedy.

OHIO

PA.

Mine Explosion ✠ •Monongah

MD.

WEST
VIRGINIA

Washington,
D.C.

•Charleston

VIRGINIA

KY.

0          100 Miles

The coal mining regions of Pennsylvania, West Virginia, Ohio and Illinois were always places of despair and tragedy. Even before the turn of the century, newspapers gave grim and lurid accounts of conditions in the mining camps.

One of the most graphic of all accounts appeared in the *New York Journal* in 1897, written by Alfred Henry Lewis, who had just completed a tour of the mining country.

"What I saw would have dissolved an angel or made a fiend to weep," he wrote. "Being neither the supernatural one nor the other, I fear I sought the profane relief of oaths as men do who find themselves in sight of outrage and cruel wrong they are helpless to redress. It was all, all horrible. Nor would I have believed that such things were in this country of America if I had not seen them. The memory, even, is like a tale told by a devil."

And speaking of the miner himself, Lewis added:

"These 95,000 slaves of the lamp are . . . the breadwinners for full 300,000 of our people. And what I set down as of hardship and starvation and overriding wrong in the grimy cases I have visited, exists also in devil's duplicate throughout all coal mining regions."

Ten years later, at a place called Monongah, in West Virginia, the full horror of mining camp conditions would be forever etched in the public mind, like bold letters written in coal dust on a white-washed wall.

It was the blackest morning of all, that morning of December 6, 1907, when 363 miners went into the pits and only one came back. In the annals of the coal industry, the disaster at Monongah remains a symbol of death that helped bring about a new regard for the life of the miner.

In 1907, Monongah was a town of about 3,000, sprawled along both banks of the West Fork River. It was a coal town, and with coal the nation's main source of power and energy, Monongah was a boom town.

"People came from far and wide," said one longtime resident. "The rough element came with the others and sometimes you could see fighting in all directions."

Starting about 5:30 on that morning of December 6, the men of Monongah—Irish, German, Italian, Greek, Slav, Pole, Hungarian—began trudging down the dark slopes to the Fairmont Coal Company's Nos. 6 and 8 connecting pits. Open carbide lamps were perched on their caps. They carried lunch pails in one hand, while shovels dangled from pick axes thrown over their shoulders.

None saw the day dawn crisp and clear.

They already were at work deep in the bowels of the mines.

It was highly dangerous work in those days. With the open flames of their carbide lamps cutting the gloom, the men drilled holes in the coal seams and filled them with black powder to blast the coal loose. They tamped the powder down with highly explosive coal dust.

Mrs. James McKain, wife of a mine inspector, recalled years later that she was in her house near the mine when "there was an awful roaring noise." Running into the yard of her home, she saw huge clouds of dust and smoke rising from both the Nos. 6 and 8 openings.

At 10:28 A.M., an explosion of cyclonic force had ripped through the two mines. Monongah's buildings tottered, and the detonation could be heard eight miles away. Even horses outside the mine were knocked down by the concussion.

In that instant, 362 miners perished in the worst coal mine disaster in the nation's history.

Mrs. McKain's husband was an inspector for the old Monongah Company from which Fairmont Coal had leased the 23,000-acre tract where Nos. 6 and 8 were located. He recalled later that coal dust was shoe-top deep in parts of No. 8 mine the day before the explosion.

A fire boss, who McKain never saw alive again, had assured him that it would be watered down that night. McKain was scheduled to inspect No. 6 the next day—and so he told his wife as he left home—but at the last moment there was a change of instructions and he went instead to another mine nearby.

Seconds after the blast, McKain ran to the No. 6 mine, in anguish. His brother, Charles, had been working inside the tunnel. About 4,000 feet from the entrance, McKain found his brother, toppled over in an equipment room.

"His lunch pail and his boots were still resting on the motor box of the machine he'd been working," McKain said. "They weren't even moved, but my brother was dead."

Rescue work began quickly. But the rescuers found only horror.

"More than 100 bodies were located in what is known as Chamber E," ran an account in the *Pittsburgh Dispatch*. "This small area represented an appalling spectacle. Dante's *Inferno* could not surpass it for horrors.

"Huddled together in a compact mass were fragments of bodies of 100 strong-

**R**escue workers maintain a feverish pace outside the No. 8 entrance as the search for survivors goes on the day after the blast. Cause of the explosion was never determined, but it set off a movement which resulted in greater safety measures.

**A** Monongah street, lined with coffins, becomes a temporary morgue in the aftermath of the mine disaster. Many of the blast-mutilated victims remained unclaimed for several days after the explosion.

hearted breadwinners. They were in all conceivable shapes and positions with hands and arms lying promiscuously around the chamber. . . ."

Only one man escaped from the mine. He was Peter Urban, who had brought his family to the United States from Poland only the preceding July.

Urban and his twin brother, working together in No. 8, managed somehow to escape the full force of the blast and ran to a "toad hole," a puncture in the surface of the ground used for air. Peter Urban was pulled to safety by rescuers. His brother, however, was dead by the time they got him to the surface.

A temporary morgue, one of several, was set up near a mine entry using tents supplied by the National Guard, and a young captain in charge never forgot the grisly scene.

His name: Matthew M. Neely, later congressman, governor and longtime U.S. senator from West Virginia. He was to build a reputation as a persistent champion of progressive mining legislation.

In a graphic speech given on the Senate floor in 1952, Neely described the scene at Monongah: "The tents were soon filled with the lifeless bodies of ghastly men. There were bodies without arms; bodies without legs; bodies without heads; and heads without bodies."

Jim McKain's wife spent the kind of day only women who have men in the mines can experience.

"She thought I was at No. 6," McKain said. "She didn't know differently until I walked into the house late that night to find her sitting in a rocking chair, crying." He hadn't been able to take time to notify his wife that he was safe.

By December 12, all workings at the mines had been ventilated, searched and 337 bodies recovered. In the following week, 17 others were found. Eight more were removed as fallen rock was cleaned up. Scores of dead were so horribly mutilated they were

Photos courtesy of United Mine Workers

never identified.

There were widely publicized reports at the time that the Monongah death toll was considerably higher than the official figure. One gravedigger insisted it ran as high as 620.

"Pure poppycock," said McKain. "We got them all out and the official figure is right. If so much as a hand or a bit of flesh could be seen beneath a fall, we recovered it."

A coroner's jury couldn't agree on the cause of the disaster, and found no negligence on the company's part, but the tragedy at Monongah, as well as the deaths of more than 3,000 other miners across the nation that year, led to improved safety standards and other technological advances.

Shortly after the Monongah explosion, the connecting of underground mines became illegal in West Virginia. And in 1910, the United States Bureau of Mines was established.

Under the rules of state and federal agencies, black powder is no longer permitted in mines. The tamping of explosives with coal dust is banned, and many other safety devices were developed to help prevent another Monongah.

Today, the veins of the old Monongah mine are empty, its years of yield over and its entrances sealed.

There is no bronze or marble memorial to the Monongah dead. But something far more fitting was erected: The St. Barbara's Memorial Nursing Home, designed as a haven for the aged and infirm survivors of those who died in the Monongah blast.

There are others who prefer to regard the progress made in coal mine safety since that fateful morning as a spiritual memorial to the victims.

Not too many years ago, the *United Mine Workers Journal* said: "Today, we can look back to the memory of those men and their grieving families and recognize that the terrible flames of suffering of Monongah lighted the way to the better life we now enjoy."

A 22-foot ventilator fan, right foreground, was lifted like a toy and hurled 80 feet through the air by the force of the mine explosion. *Inset:* This group of mine inspectors posed for this photograph after going into the pits to determine the cause of the Monongah explosion. Included in the group were representatives of the British and French mining industries.

**23**

# HELL'S HUNDRED ACRES

**T**he fire started on the eighth floor of the 10-story structure, which was regarded as "fireproof." Many of the victims hurled themselves from the upper floor to escape the searing flames.

The Asch Building, on Greene Street in New York City's lower Manhattan, was built in 1900. The 10-story structure was regarded as modern and fireproof.

On Saturday, March 25, 1911, the upper three floors, home of the Triangle Shirtwaist Company, hummed with activity. The company was one of a number of so-called "cloak and suit" shops which dotted the area.

On this particular day, as the first touch of spring warmed the air, there were 625 employees at work, mostly young women earning some extra Saturday money.

At 4:45 P.M., the quitting bell rang and the hundreds of workers prepared to leave for the day. In another five minutes, the building would be empty.

Suddenly, passersby heard a muffled explosion and saw black smoke pouring from the eighth floor of the Asch Building.

Within a couple of hours, the bodies of 147 employees of the Triangle Shirtwaist Company lay in orderly rows on the sidewalk.

As fire raged through the top three floors of the building, about 50 girls frantically hurled themselves out of the windows—to their deaths below. Many burned to death inside. Still others died on the building's single fire escape, as flames enveloped them as they climbed through windows, or when the fire escape buckled from the heat and weight, plunging several to their deaths in the back yard.

Still others perished on top of elevator cages when they jumped into the shaft hoping to slide down the cables.

Firemen found heaps of bodies piled

Culver Photo

against emergency doors that were kept bolted, as one newspaper explained, "to safeguard employers from the loss of goods by the departure of workers through fire exits instead of elevators."

The cause of the fire was never fully established, but it was believed to have started in an accumulation of fabric scraps on the eighth floor.

Max Rother, a Triangle tailor, was on the eighth floor when the fire started. When he heard the cry of alarm, he and the manager, Max Burnstein, grabbed pails of water in an effort to put out the blaze. But overhead racks of partially finished garments were already ablaze and their efforts were useless.

Rosie Safran, one of the survivors, provided a graphic account of her experience. She said she ran for one of the fire exits, but it was locked and a number of girls were jammed in front of it.

"If we couldn't get out we would all be roasted alive," she said. "The locked door that blocked us was half of wood; the upper half was thick glass. Some girls were screaming, some were beating the doors with their fists, some were trying to tear it open.

"Someone broke out the glass part of the door with something hard and heavy. I climbed or was pulled through the broken glass and ran downstairs to the sixth floor, where someone took me down to the street.

"I got out to the street and watched the upper floors burning, and the girls hanging by their hands and then dropping as the fire reached them. There they were, dead on the sidewalk. It was an awful, awful sight, especially to me who had so many friends among the girls and young men who were being roasted alive or dashed to death."

Thousands of spectators who crowded into the area watched in horror as a 13-year-old girl hung by her fingertips to the sill of a tenth-story window. A tongue of flame burned her fingers and she dropped to her death.

Another girl threw her pocketbook, then her hat, then her coat from a tenth-floor window. A moment later, her body came whirling after them to death.

On the ninth floor, a man and woman appeared at a window. The man embraced the woman and kissed her. Then he hurled her to the street and jumped. Both were killed.

Five girls stood together at the tenth-floor windows as they waited for fire ladders to reach them. The ladders fell two stories short. The five girls, clinging to one another and with flames streaming from their hair and clothing, leaped together and lay broken in a misshapen heap on the pavement below.

Another girl waved a handkerchief to

**O**ne of the work rooms at the clothing manufacturing firm after the fire. All that remained were charred walls and work benches.

the crowd before she jumped from one of the upper floors. Her burning dress caught on a wire and the crowd watched her hang there until her dress burned free and she came toppling down.

Several eyewitnesses reported seeing people jumping from the burning building even before the first fire trucks had arrived.

Benjamin Levy was at work in his nearby offices when he heard someone report a fire around the corner.

"I rushed downstairs and when I reached the sidewalk," he said, "the girls were already jumping from the windows. None of them moved after they struck the sidewalk.

"Several men ran up with a net which they got somewhere and I seized one side of it to help them hold it," he said. "It was about 10 feet square and we managed to catch about 15 girls. I don't believe we saved more than one or two, however. The fall was so great that they bounced to the sidewalk after striking the net.

"Bodies were falling all around us and two or three of the men with me were knocked down. The girls just leaped wildly out of the windows and turned over and over before reaching the sidewalk.

"One girl held back after all the rest and clung to the window casing until the flames from the window below crept up to her and set her clothing on fire. Then she jumped far over the net and was killed instantly . . . like all the rest."

Inside the flaming structure, many victims sought escape via the solitary elevator which was in service. They crowded around the elevator shaft but no cars responded to their frantic ringing. Time after time, they saw the elevator approach the eighth floor, fill up with passengers and go down again. Girls who rushed to the staircase were met by flames.

Elevator operator Joseph Zito said that on his last trip down he could hear the thud of bodies hitting the top of his car as trapped workers jumped from the upper floors after giving up hope of rescue. In the other elevator shaft, more than 30 bodies would be counted as they piled up on the floor.

By 7 P.M., the flames were out, and the grim task of removing the dead—many burned beyond recognition—was begun.

As firemen started lowering the charred remains in basket slings from the upper floors, the scene was more than one coroner's office worker could stand.

Weeping openly, he cried: "These poor girls were carried up in the elevator to work in the morning—now they come down at the end of a rope."

As each victim was brought out, anguished wailings could be heard from the crowd. Pet names spoken in Yiddish and Italian rose in shrill agony above the deeper moan of the throng.

Rhinelander Waldo, then New York City fire commissioner, would declare: "The loss of more than 140 lives resulting from the fire . . . has demonstrated forcibly the contention of the fire department that while buildings may be fireproof, the contents are not."

By the standards of the time, the owners of the Triangle Shirtwaist Company were not accountable for the tragedy, despite evidence that they had skimped on safety precautions.

Ironically, only nine days before the holocaust, the possible fire dangers that lurked in these garment industry sweatshops were discussed in a New York City newspaper article.

The Triangle tragedy alerted a previously indifferent public to shocking factory conditions that had been ignored or condoned and a clamor went up for reform.

Many present-day regulations regarding factory inspection, fireproofing and sprinkler systems are largely traceable to the Triangle tragedy.

Yet, 50 years later, when the International Ladies Garment Workers Union held a memorial at the old Asch Building, Fire Commissioner Edward Cavanagh, Jr., said that "50 years or 50 decades will not dim the horror or tragedy of fire."

Nothing that a number of fires in that area during the intervening years had cost the lives of firemen and workers, he called that section of the city "Hell's 100 Acres" and said the "shadow of another Triangle" continued to loom.

**B**odies of dead from the Triangle fire were placed in temporary coffins at the morgue to await identification. The tragedy alerted a previously indifferent public to shocking factory conditions.

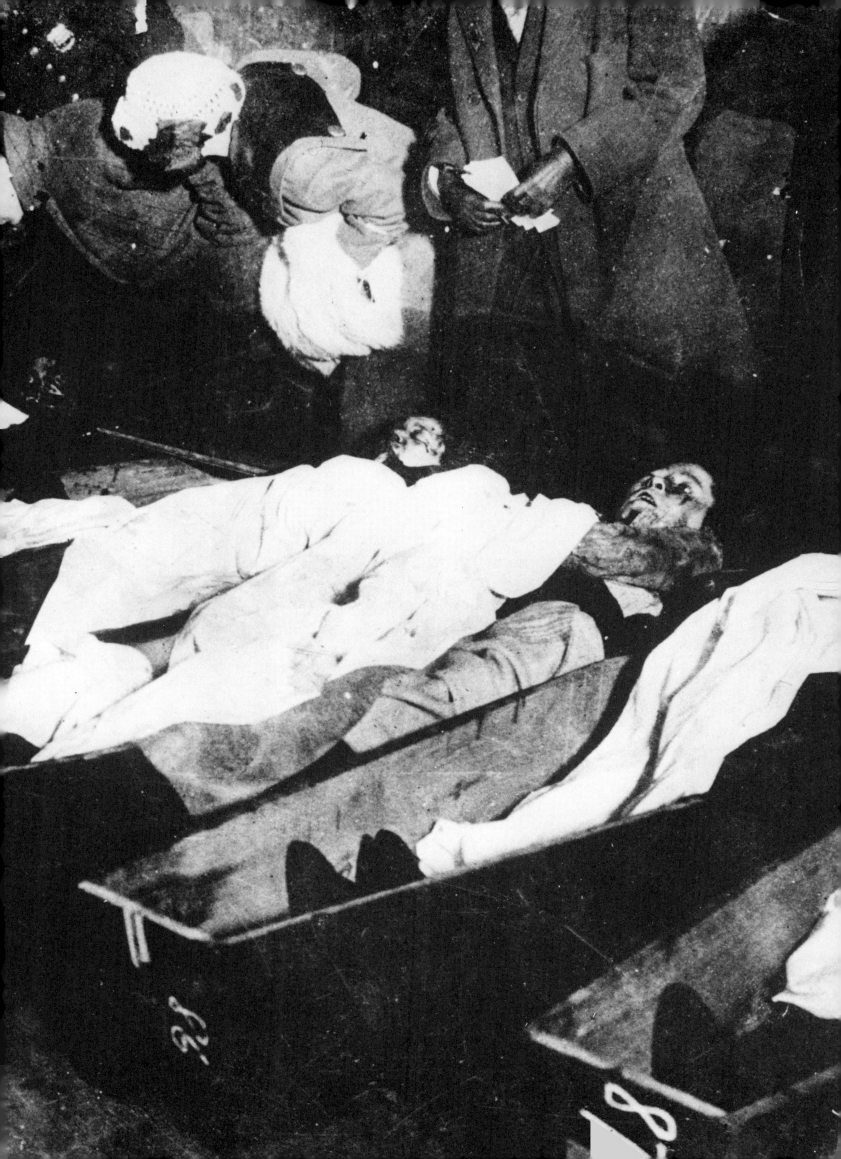

# DEATH TAKES AN OUTING

**T**he *Eastland* overturned at its berth in the Chicago River and 812 men, women and children lost their lives. About 2,500 were aboard when the ship capsized.

GRAND ST.

Eastland
Capsized

Chicago River

LAKE ST.

CHICAGO

City
Hall

CLARK ST.

STATE ST.

MICHIGAN AVE.

Grant
Park

Art
Institute

JACKSON BLVD.

0          ¼ Mile

LOOP

She was known as a "cranky" ship. But the *Eastland* had seen 12 years of service on the Great Lakes and could steam at a reputed 30 knots or so per hour, making her one of the fastest ships in the Lakes area.

Surely, she was the most impressive looking of five steamers berthed on the Chicago River just west of the Clark Street Bridge. The *Eastland* was a trim three-decker, 265 feet long and weighing nearly 2,000 tons.

It was the morning of Saturday, July 24, 1915, and a happy crowd of 7,000 people—employees of the Western Electric Co. and their families—were waiting to board the *Eastland* and the four other ships for the company's annual outing to Michigan City and the Indiana dune country.

It was only natural that most of the pic-nickers, especially the children, were hoping to board the biggest and the best of the steamers: the *Eastland*.

Reports had cropped up at various times that the *Eastland* was not as safe as she appeared to be.

Built in 1903 by the Jenks Shipbuilding Co. at Port Huron, Michigan, the twin-screw, steel-hulled vessel had undergone renovation a year later. Her owners had her upper works expanded in order to accommodate more passengers.

But because *Eastland*'s hull was light, her superstructure heavy and her shape too narrow for her height, she soon got the reputation of being a "cranky" ship, a ship plagued with instability.

In fact, on several occasions, crewmen had to herd frightened passengers to one side of the vessel in order to correct a dangerous list on the opposite side.

But danger was the farthest thing in the minds of men, women and children clambering on board and swarming to the topmost deck where they could wave to their friends and catch a glimpse of the Chicago skyline.

And danger was the farthest thing in the mind of *Eastland*'s master, Captain Harry Pedersen, as he made plans to get underway. Although he may have been mildly concerned about the slight list to starboard where passengers had loaded, Captain Pedersen was certain that inspectors would not allow boarders to exceed the ship's 2,500-person capacity.

He ordered the engineer to trim ship by partially filling the port ballast tanks. *Eastland*'s bow line was freed, and the ship drifted sideways into the river, its stern line still fastened to the dock.

After making secure a hawser from the tug *Kenosha, Eastland* suddenly listed sharply to port, but soon righted itself.

*Eastland* again heeled over to port and hundreds of passengers started sliding across the sloping deck, canted at almost a 45-degree slant. Crew members tried to drive the panicked passengers back to starboard, but the incline already was too steep for them.

Hundreds of passengers below deck also were thrown into panic and they started clawing one another in an effort to make it up the companionways.

Then the worst happened.

The weight of the *Eastland*'s list snapped the stern line and the ship rolled over.

**T**he steamer *Eastland,* pride of the Great Lakes, was a "cranky" ship. Although she was the focus of one of the greatest maritime disasters in American history, she was later raised (*inset*), repaired and sold to the government. During World War II, she served as a naval training ship.

**T**he end of an outing. The steamer *Eastland* is shown on its side, several days after it capsized at its berth in the Chicago River.

Captain Pedersen said later: "I was on the bridge and was about ready to pull out when I noticed the boat begin to list. I shouted orders to open the gangway to give the people a chance to get out. The ship continued to roll over on its side and was drifting toward the middle of the river. When she went over I jumped and held onto the upper side. It all happened in two minutes . . . I don't know how it happened."

The anguished cries of the crowd on shore mingled with the screams of the *Eastland*'s passengers as hundreds were thrown into the turgid waters of the Chicago River.

Children bobbed like corks in the water, then disappeared; some passengers started swimming to shore; others who could not swim screamed in terror before going under.

Peter Vehan, who saw his sweetheart, Mary Kesel, swept to her death, said, "We were on the starboard side of the boat and slid to the port side when the list came. Scores of chairs and tables piled up on us and forced us apart. One chair struck Mary on the head. She was unconscious when she fell into the water. I tried my best to get her side, but she disappeared. I searched about in the water for her, but she never came up."

Theodore Soderstrom, who lost his wife when both were thrown into the river, said that passengers were crowded 10 to 30 deep on the outer rail of the ship.

"I noticed the boat beginning to career slightly, but at first it gave me no uneasiness. Then just before we pulled out, several hundred passengers who had been saying good-bye to persons on the dock came over to the port rail. Almost instantly the boat lurched drunkenly, righted itself, and then pitched once more," Soderstrom said.

"By this time passengers knew there was something wrong," he said. "But it all happened so quickly that no one knew what to do. For a third time the boat lurched, this time slowly, and there were screams as everyone tried to get to the side of the vessel next to the dock.

"Many were beaten down to the deck unconscious in this mad rush. Probably a dozen persons—it might have been more—jumped into the water. But they were crushed under the side of the boat before they had a chance to swim away."

Many acts of heroism were recorded.

One policeman, Harry H. Loesher, jumped into a rowboat and was able to get about 50 people ashore in repeated trips.

One unknown hero, underneath the pier near the overturned vessel, clung to a piling and rescued two women and three children before weakening under the ordeal and drowning.

Another man wrapped a rope around his waist, swam out and rescued 25. Later, rescuers using acetylene torches and electric drills found a few passengers alive below decks. More than 80 bodies were pulled from the wreckage.

Of the estimated 2,500 happy picnickers who climbed onto *Eastland*'s gangway, 812 people found that death took an outing with them. The victims included 22 entire families.

Most observers immediately blamed the tragedy on crowding at the port rails. But some Chicago officials thought that was too pat an answer and ordered the arrest of Captain Pedersen and his first mate, Dell Fisher.

Both men were almost lynched by an angry crowd of almost 10,000 as they were being taken to City Hall.

In the aftermath of the disaster, there were varying opinions as to whom was actually to blame.

Evidence produced at the official inquiry pointed a finger of negligence at the *Eastland*'s owners as well as maritime officials who had reports of the ship's instability on earlier occasions.

Also blamed were the original shipbuilders as well as Captain Pedersen and various members of the crew.

But the bitterest pill to swallow for survivors and families of victims came 20 years later when the courts held *Eastland*'s owners blameless and declared that *Eastland* was seaworthy.

Blame was laid on the head of the ship's engineer, who, the courts said, made a mistake by over-filling the ballast tanks.

The final chapter of this troubled ship didn't end until 1946.

After the tragedy, the overturned vessel was raised, repaired and sold to the federal government. Rechristened as the U.S.S. *Wilmette,* she served as a naval training ship until towed up the Chicago River and scrapped.

The body of a woman passenger is hauled from below decks by firemen and other rescuers. She was one of many who perished when the excursion steamer overturned in the Chicago River.

The Chicago River tugboat *Kenosha* was able to rescue hundreds by providing a floating platform to shore.

# HOLOCAUST ON THE HIGH SEAS

**S**till-smoking hulk of luxury liner *Morro Castle* is shown washed up on the beach behind Convention Hall in Asbury Park, New Jersey.

NEW
JERSEY

PA.

New
York

Atlantic

Ocean

Asbury
Park

Morro Castle
Fire

Philadelphia

0                    40 Miles

The fast and luxurious Ward Line passenger ship *Morro Castle* was bucking a stiff nor'easter off the New Jersey coast the night of September 7, 1934.

The *Morro Castle* was about to complete another Havana-New York pleasure cruise. By dawn, it would reach quarantine and then sail up New York Harbor to its pier.

But a pall had fallen on the ship that final night at sea. At suppertime, Captain Robert Wilmott had been found in his bathtub, dead of an apparent heart attack. With the master of the ship gone, command fell to the nervous first mate, William F Warms. Last night festivities were cancelled and by 2:30 A.M. only a few diehards among the 321 passengers were still drinking in the smoking room and in the lounge. It was then someone noticed a wisp of smoke curling out of a locker in the writing room.

Within a short time, much of the 11,520-ton *Morro Castle* was a mass of flames. And of the 548 passengers and crewmen aboard, 134 were to meet their doom by drowning or by incineration in the floating crematorium.

The burning of the *Morro Castle* was not the worst marine tragedy ever recorded in terms of lost lives.

But now, over 50 years later, the disaster still stands as one of the strangest, saddest and most shameful in seafaring history. It left a record of incredible ineptitude of officers and men, of tragic hysteria and heart-rending helplessness of passengers, of occasional heroism and prevailing cowardice.

Shortly after the first wisp of smoke was spotted, a small blaze erupted in the writing room and was fought by stay-up passengers and three stewards.

Their efforts to extinguish the blaze were unsuccessful and within minutes, the magnificent vessel had become a roaring furnace. The flames were fanned by brisk winds which reached an intensity of 40 knots when the ship headed into them. Over the beat of engines, the crash of the waves and

**T**he fast and luxurious passenger liner *Morro Castle* burns off the New Jersey coast in the tragic end of a Havana-New York pleasure cruise. Of the 548 passengers and crewmen, 134 lost their lives on the floating furnace or drowned.

the howling of the wind rose the screams of men, women and children.

The tragedy was one of confusion, negligence and stupidity.

Only perfunctory fire drills had been held during the voyage so as not to alarm the passengers. Discipline among crewmen generally was poor. The bosun, for example, who should have led the fire fighters, was drunk in his bunk.

Passengers and crew were not aroused until the ship was already doomed. Some passengers were trapped in their smoke-filled or blazing rooms and died protesting with shrill shrieks of pain or panic. Several had passed out at drunken private parties and probably passed out of this world without every knowing what happened.

Even longer was the delay in sending out an SOS. Time after time, Second Radio Operator George I. Alagna had made the 50-foot trip from the radio shack to the bridge to get instructions from Acting Captain Warms to tap out a distress call. Each time, Alagna would testify later, he was ignored by the stunned first mate who paced and mumbled, "Am I dreaming, or is it true?"

Waiting in the radio room for a message from the bridge was George W. Rogers, the pudgy, genial chief operator. A wet towel was wrapped around the lower part of his face to allow him to breathe in the stifling smoke. His feet were propped on the rungs of his chair to keep them off the hot deck.

A nearby ship and Coast Guard station saw and reported the fire aboard *Morro Castle* before 3:23 A.M., when Acting Captain Warms finally gave permission to transmit an SOS. One minute later would have been too late for most on board.

Chief Engineer Eban S. Abbott put on his dress uniform, went halfway down to the smoke-filled engine room, thought better of it and returned to the deck where he and 28 other crew members and only three passengers scrambled into the No. 1 lifeboat and

**C**hief Radio Operator George W. Rogers, who was first hailed as the hero of the *Morro Castle*. Rogers was to die in prison years later as a convicted murderer.

The charred remains of a lifeboat, still hanging on its davits aboard *Morro Castle,* offers mute testimony to the ferocity of the fire that swept the liner—and to one of the most shameful chapters in seafaring history.

A lightly loaded lifeboat with survivors of *Morro Castle* nears rescue ship *Monarch of Bermuda.* The *Monarch* brought one dead woman and about 80 survivors into New York City.

shoved off for shore—steering through struggling swimmers but not stopping to pick them up. (In fact, the first five half-empty lifeboats of a total of six that reached shore carried 92 members of the crew but only six passengers.)

Abbott's gang on duty below worked heroically to the last minute, and barely escaped to the dangers on deck.

But it was evident that a large percentage of *Morro Castle*'s crew knew little or nothing about their emergency duties. Fire doors, which might have contained the blaze, remained wide open, sucking in fire-fanning drafts. And essential firefighting equipment had been removed or was inoperable.

In the meantime, the ship was steered over an erratic course, with the wind blowing the flames first in one direction, then another. Eventually, the steering apparatus malfunctioned, then the engines stopped and the lights went out. No area remained safe; the decks were too hot to stand on and the railings raised blisters to the touch. Gunpowder used for certain ship operations blew up in a frightening explosion.

The darkness of the deck and, later, the glow of red hot metal and rising flames became the backdrop for scores of scenes, tender and terrible:

Aging couples and newlyweds embracing, then, hand in hand, leaping into the cold, black water . . . the shooting of a looting seaman . . . a New York cop, with drawn pistol, telling a sailor who was about to precede passengers down a rope into a lifeboat, "You're a dead man, if you jump" . . . a Bronx priest striding along the decks giving absolution to passengers and crew while a seaman walked beside him solicitously bathing the priest's burned face with a damp cloth . . . a mother pushing her 8-year-old son into the sea to save him from the fire—but never to see him again . . . fights for precious lifebelts . . . a stout blonde woman,

her hips stuck in the porthole of the blazing cabin, screaming for help . . . human torches . . . men and women clinging desperately to ropes hanging from empty lifeboat davits and, as they tired, dropping one by one into the ocean . . . prayers, curses and shrieks.

There were other piteous episodes in the water. Couples who had plunged over the side holding hands were now wrenched apart and swept away by massive waves. Young men and women tried to help their parents remain afloat. Lightly loaded lifeboats steered a non-stop course through the living, the dying and the dead who bobbed on the surface of the heaving ocean. There also were sharks.

A score of small boats from New Jersey fishing villages headed through the scud and the squalls to haul survivors onto the narrow decks. The dead were stacked aboard like cordwood. Lifeboats from three nearby steamers picked up some of the others. A few people made it to shore on their own, sometimes sharing the same life jacket. Some of the dead were still floating onto the breakers ashore almost a week after the tragedy.

The *Morro Castle,* abandoned by all except Acting Captain Warms and a small group of sailors huddled on the bow of the stricken ship, was taken under tow by a smaller Coast Guard vessel. The tow broke and the still smoking gutted skeleton was washed up on the beach behind Convention Hall at Asbury Park, New Jersey.

Thousands of people came to stare at the hideous hulk. At one time, you could see the wreck for 25 cents, with a sign proclaiming that the proceeds were "for the benefit of the dead families."

The *Morro Castle* became scrap iron. The Ward Line, fined $10,000 for negligence, later became the Ward-Garcia Line, which operated charter ships under a foreign flag. Warms and Chief Engineer Abbott were

**E**nd of a holiday: a dying passenger from *Morro Castle* is carried ashore by lifeguards at Sea Girt, New Jersey. He died soon after drifting ashore from burning liner. This passenger jumped overboard wearing only underwear and life belt.

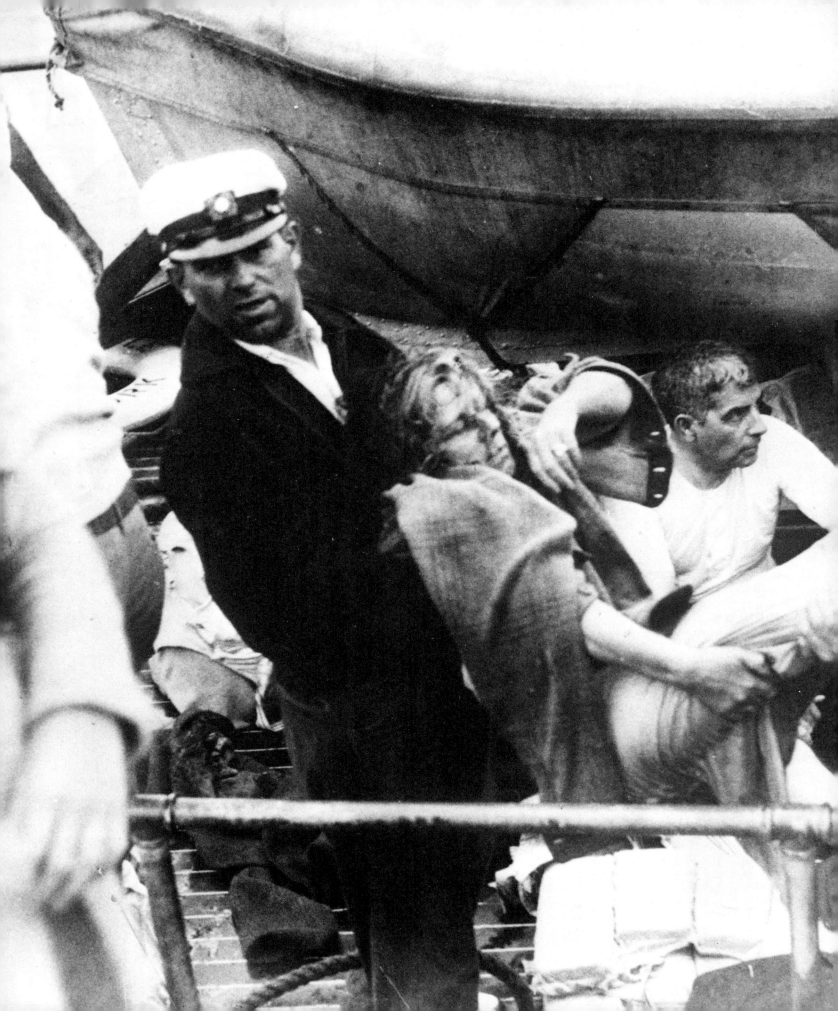

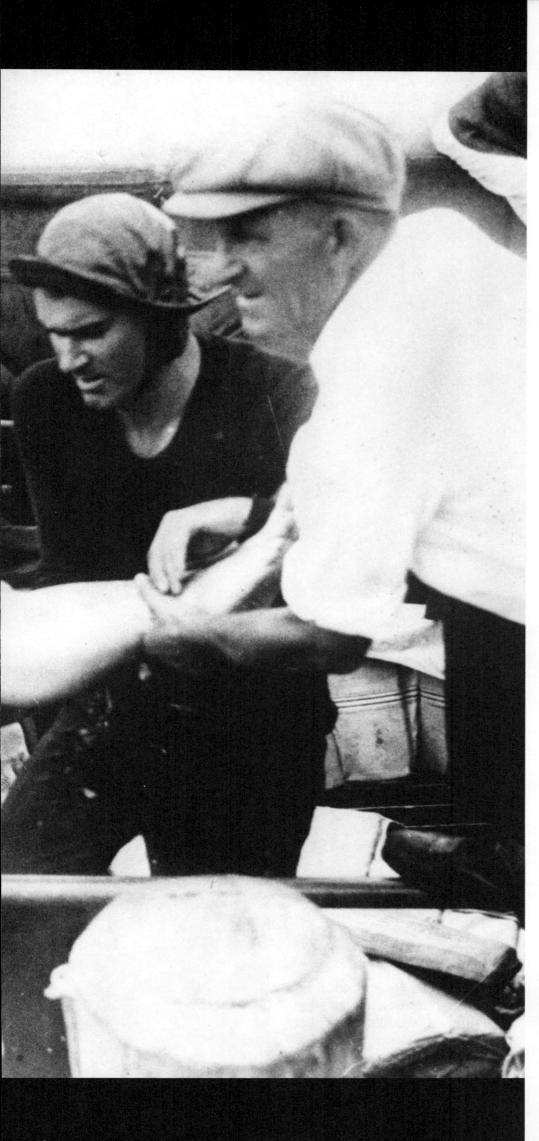

convicted of negligence, but their convictions later were reversed and the Federal Circuit Court of Appeals opined that Warms had "lived up to the best tradition of the sea."

The claims of injured survivors and heirs of the dead were settled, with awards ranging from nothing to $62,000 and averaging $8,530. Investigating boards made their recommendations for safer ships.

But the strangest episode to emerge from the sad saga of the *Morro Castle* centered around Chief Radio Operator Rogers, who, at the time, appeared as a particular hero of the affair. He had stayed at his post under frightful conditions of fiery danger. Later, he was paraded through his hometown of Bayonne, New Jersey, given dinners and medals and he even made a vaudeville tour to tell about his scorching experience.

A chain of circumstances later indicated that the whole ghastly affair may have been the deliberate work of one man: George Rogers.

It was found that Rogers had a history of crime dating back to the age of 12. His record included several arrests for sodomy, theft and suspicion of arson.

After the disaster, Rogers joined the Bayonne police as a radio repairman. In 1938 he was convicted of trying to blow up his immediate superior with an ingenious bomb. He was paroled during World War II, but in 1953 he was convicted in the bludgeon deaths of an elderly printer and his spinster daughter and sent to prison for life.

Rogers died in prison in 1958, to a chorus of obituaries mourning the hero of the *Morro Castle* who had gone bad.

The exact cause of Captain Wilmott's death on the eve of the fire was never quite established. Some speculate that Rogers may have poisoned him.

But the *Morro Castle* was also Captain Wilmott's funeral pyre. All that was ever found of him for post-mortem examination were some scattered ashes and a few small bone fragments.

**A** woman survivor of *Morro Castle,* weak from exposure, is taken off a small fishing boat at Manasquan, New Jersey, the morning after the fire.

**47**

# IT TOOK ONLY A SPARK

This is the New London Independent School, called the "world's richest school," as it stood before the disaster. The explosion demolished the $300,000 structure.

**A**n explosion of natural gas turned the Independent School into a pile of rubble. Here, rescue workers from the East Texas oil fields comb through the wreckage for survivors.

49

The New London, Texas, Independent School, a handsome two-story brick structure once called the richest school in the world, was located in the heart of the East Texas oil fields, about 120 miles southeast of Dallas and about 70 miles from the Louisiana border.

On its grounds, seven oil wells, owned by the school district, pumped wealth into its coffers. The horizon surrounding the school was a forest of pumping wells; and burning gas flares lit the night sky.

Its students, mostly children of oil-field workers, came from communities as far away as 15 miles from New London, a town born in the feverish oil activity of 1930–31.

On Thursday, March 18, 1937, at about 3:15 P.M., some elementary classes at the school already had been dismissed and the children had either left for home or were playing on the school grounds while they awaited buses.

School officials earlier in the afternoon had debated whether to let the other pupils leave school a half-hour earlier than usual to attend a track meet, but they had rejected the idea.

An estimated 600 students still remained in the building, and in a gymnasium a short distance away, mothers gathered for a P.T.A. meeting.

Mrs. Kenneth Marshall was then a 17-year-old high school senior in economics class at the time. Twelve-year-old Geneace Humphres had skipped her music class to watch a boys' volleyball game in the school yard. And Billie Sue Hall, a fifth-grader, stooped under her desk to get some paper.

In the basement of the school, a natural gas line that fed the school heating system had developed a leak and gas had slowly filled every nook and cranny. The accumulated odorless gas needed only a tiny spark to set off its explosive power and bring catastrophe. At that moment, a manual training teacher walked over to an electric switch on the shop wall. He grasped the handle and thrust it upward to start one of the machines for the students to use.

Suddenly, a low rumble rolled beneath the floor of the building. Then came a tremendous blast. The walls buckled. The floor

**R**escue workers dig through the ruins of the Independent School. The blast killed 296 persons, most of them children. *Inset:* The force of the blast hurled large chunks of the building into nearby areas. This automobile standing nearby was crumpled by falling debris. Luckily, no one was inside to be injured.

surged up in huge concrete slabs. The roof lifted, then collapsed.

And in the rubble lay the bodies of 280 children, 14 teachers and two mothers, killed in the worst school disaster of this century.

"There was no warning," Mrs. Marshall recalled. "Nothing. Just a tremendous explosion. I felt like I was crushed to death from the pressure.

"I found myself outside. My first thought was—this is the end of the world. Everywhere there was dense smoke and pulverized brick and mortar. I can remember people were screaming and lying dead all around me but I didn't even cry.

"I wandered around the bodies. I saw a boy who lived close to us lying there impaled on an iron beam."

Geneace Humphres was jolted by the concussion. Then she saw the roof of her school mushroom upward and settle in a fog of dust which blotted out the sky. She learned that night that all 50 boys and girls as well as the teacher of the music class from which she had played hooky were killed.

And as Billie Sue Hall stooped to get some paper, the desk fell on her head. She suffered a fractured skull, but survived—one of the 10 in her class of 36 fifth-graders to do so. Billie Sue stayed in the hospital for 10 days, and during that period, her mother said, "she never cried, never said a word. She just didn't talk about it."

Within minutes after the explosion, New London was the scene of one of the nation's great rescue efforts.

Frantic parents rushed to the school and either tore pitifully at the mountains of rubble or stood by numbly while an ever-increasing army of oil-field workers and other volunteers dug into the debris looking for survivors. Huge trucks with steel cables, used in the oil fields, were pressed into rescue service. They pulled off slabs of concrete that formed the tombs of the victims.

Bill Rives of Dallas, one of the first newsmen on the scene, said that some of the children were smashed so badly that identification was impossible.

"We remember one anguished mother who went from one temporary morgue to another, carrying a bit of dress material. She

had made a dress for her daughter and the child had worn it to school that day for the first time.

"Her mother finally found the truth she dreaded—a crushed body which she knew was that of her daughter because the material matched that of the dead child's dress.

Almost every bit of available space in the New London area became a temporary morgue. Funeral parlors for miles around were utilized and some bodies were carried as far as Dallas.

One mother, who had spent the entire night visiting morgues in search of her 16-year-old daughter, finally found her in the nearby town of Overton—and dropped dead of a heart attack.

Felix R. McKnight, another newsman on the scene who would later become executive editor of the *Dallas Times-Herald,* remembered:

"As you reached the crest of a ridge near the school, you got the first view of a scene that brought tears to your eyes . . . tears that stayed for days, weeks and months. A generation of that fine oil-field community had been wiped out in a terrible few seconds.

"Brick, steel and stone had settled in a welded mass. In a matter of an hour or two, giant floodlights were erected and at nightfall the brilliance of their glare lighted a scene that still flashes through my mind.

"Men, some of them stripped to the waist, stood in long lines that fingered into the ruins and silently passed baskets filled with debris. They dug with bare and raw hands, with acetylene torches, with anything—for their own children.

"Nature made it even worse. Suddenly a violent storm broke upon the area but the digging, the bulldozing, the cutting never ceased . . . and at dawn the miracle of the men was complete. The site was almost level. The last victim had been removed."

But the roughnecks—oil-field workers—found little to console them as they dug through the rubble. They found only 85 still alive—294 had died in the explosion. Two more died later of injuries.

Now it was time to bury the dead. The children were buried in separate graves in

Scores of New London, Texas, children perished at their desks as tons of brick and mortar cascaded around them.

This pile of books tells its own story of the disaster that overtook the New London school. The young girl rummaging through them was one of the fortunate survivors.

**A** distraught father wanders among the sheeted dead, searching for the body of his daughter.

**E**leven-year-old Connie Downs miraculously survived the New London explosion. Here, her 7-year-old brother, Billy, brings her flowers as she recuperates in a Tyler, Texas, hospital.

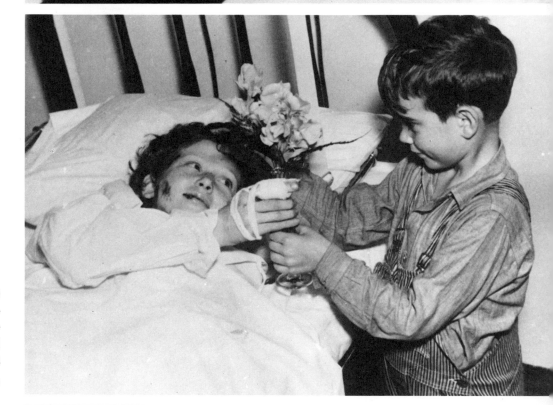

**M**rs. Tom Rodgers gives comfort to her son as he lies on a hospital bed. The youngster, pulled battered and bleeding from the wreckage of his school, also survived the disaster.

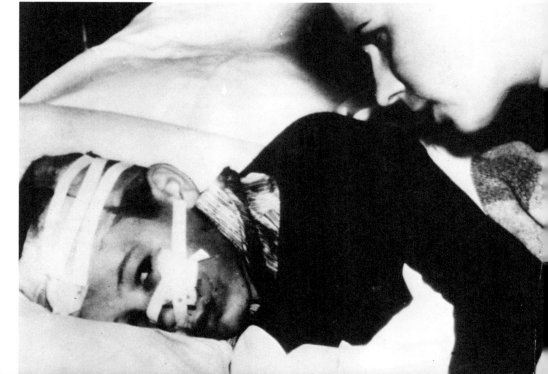

nearby Pleasant Hill, and for several days there was an almost constant procession to the cemetery.

Later, investigators would report that the explosion was due to a combination of circumstances. Besides the leak in the gas line, contributing factors were poor ventilation in the basement area, the use of odorless oil-well gas and the overly complex heating system installed in the $300,000 school.

No one person was responsible for the tragedy, investigators added. "It was the collective faults of average individuals, ignorant of or indifferent to the need of precautionary measures, where they cannot, in their lack of knowledge, visualize a danger or hazard."

Immediately after the tragedy, President Roosevelt, who was vacationing in Warm Springs, Georgia, at the time, called on the Red Cross and all government agencies "to stand by and render every assistance in their power to the community to which this shocking tragedy has come."

The morning after the disaster, New London received an overseas cable which read: "My people join in sending sympathy in the loss of your flowering youth." It was signed—Adolf Hitler.

School was resumed 11 days later in whatever space could be found in New London, but of the 1,200 children still able to attend, only 287 reported on that first day. Many parents kept their children at home, still in near-shock from the recent disaster.

A new school was built on the site and erected nearby was a tall cenotaph, a memorial to the victims of one of the worst child disasters in the nation's history.

Twenty-two years after the disaster, newsman McKnight returned to the scene to write: "Today, the real monument stands proud and unbreakable in the East Texas valley. A new school, a new generation, a new faith."

But some of the rescuers could recall something else written on one of the blackboards dug out of the debris of the New London Independent School:

"Oil and natural gas are East Texas' greatest blessing. Without them, this school would not be here and none of us would be here learning our lessons."

There were not enough hearses to bear the dead to their final resting place so pickup trucks were enlisted instead.

# THE END OF AN ERA

**N**ew Yorkers got this rare glimpse of the *Hindenburg* as she passed over the city on what would be her last voyage.

NEW
JERSEY

N. Y.

New York

Atlantic
Ocean

Trenton

Hindenburg
Explosion

Lakehurst

0                    40 Miles

On May 6, 1937, President Franklin Roosevelt was fishing off the Texas coast. His son, Elliott, caught a tarpon that day.

Good golf balls were 46 cents each and figure skater Maribel Vincent, nine times North American champion, announced she was turning pro. The play "Tobacco Road" was in its fourth year on Broadway.

And in Lakehurst, New Jersey, the dirigible *Hindenburg* was due to complete her first flight of the season.

Three days earlier, 36 had boarded the airship in Frankfurt, Germany, for the first of 18 trips planned that year for the *Hindenburg* by her owners, the Zeppelin Transport Company. Since going into service in 1936, the *Hindenburg*—named for the former German general and president Paul von Hindenburg—had made 37 crossings to North and South America, carrying 3,059 passengers in elegant comfort nearly 210,000 miles.

For their $400 fare, the travellers got not only a luxurious two or three days aloft, but also a unique experience.

Four chefs prepared continental meals on board from a larder stocked with lobsters, fowl and roasts. The wine list covered a page. There was a lounge and a bar and 70 staterooms.

On B deck, passengers were able to take a shower replenished by water distilled from the air. Charles E. Rosendahl, commander of the Naval Air Station at Lakehurst, said the shower spray was "more like a seltzer bottle than the shower at the 'Y,'" but it was a sumptuous advance in air travel.

There had never been anything to match travel on an airship. The four diesel engines were so far aft that the passengers could scarcely hear them. There was hardly any motion as the huge ship, nearly a sixth of a mile long, "floated" over the ocean. In fair weather, the big windows of the gondola were left open.

The trips were long enough for passengers to develop cordiality, but short enough to keep nerves from rubbing. The crew shared the adventure with passengers, who were taken on tours through the ship. Captain Ernst Lehmann, who was along as an advisor, would sign menus. Passenger Joseph Spah once told him he had been in three flying accidents. "Don't worry, my friend," Lehmann replied. "Zeppelins never have accidents."

Surely, none was expected, with such a vigilant crew aboard. A steward even took a wind-up toy away from some children because it shot off sparks.

There was a smoking room aboard, although the 16 huge bags that lifted the airship were inflated with hydrogen, a highly flammable and hot burning gas. But as a precaution, the smoking room had a double door entrance, and the room was kept under slightly higher air pressure to prevent stray wisps of hydrogen from seeping in.

Further, all matches and cigarette lighters were confiscated on boarding. "We Germans don't fool around with hydrogen," Chief Steward Heinrich Kubis told a passenger. And they didn't.

Crewmen working inside the aluminum structure of the *Hindenburg* wore asbestos coveralls to keep buttons or belt buckles from striking a spark. The catwalks and ladders were encased in rubber.

Yet, even though hydrogen enabled the *Hindenburg* to carry 16½ additional tons, the Germans would have preferred to use helium, a gas with less lifting power. Helium was a rare gas in that it didn't burn. Rarer still was that it was found in commercially feasible amounts in but one country in the world—the United States.

Germany hadn't directly asked for helium, probably because it knew what the answer might be. Washington wasn't going to part with an asset that might give military advantage to a nation led by Adolf Hitler.

But if the passengers boarding that day at Frankfurt, Germany, had any qualms, they could reflect on the record of the company's other dirigible, the *Graf Zeppelin*. She had carried 13,000 passengers over a million miles since her maiden flight in 1928.

**C**aptain Max Pruss, commander of the *Hindenburg*.

The latest *Collier's Magazine,* due on the stands the same day the *Hindenburg* was due at Lakehurst, said, "Only a stroke of war or an unfathomable act of God will ever mar this German dirigible's passenger safety record."

The *Hindenburg* took off routinely from Frankfurt although the band playing farewell music scattered when the wind drifted the 804-foot airship their way.

Captain Max Pruss, a veteran of airships, was in command. Captain Lehmann, who had commanded the *Hindenburg* the year before and was along as an advisor, didn't want to go because his son had died a few days before. But he thought he might have a chance to go to Washington and talk to authorities about obtaining helium.

The passengers were a mixed lot.

There was Joseph Spah, a 32-year-old comic acrobat from Long Island, New York, whose best trick was playing a drunk hanging from a lamppost. Philip Mangone, 53, a womens' wear designer, was returning to his New York home. Years back, he had cancelled his ticket at the last minute for the liner *Lusitania's* doomed voyage.

James O'Laughlin, 28, was on his way back to Chicago after a European holiday. Margaret Mather was paying a visit to her professor brother at Princeton University. Peter Belin, 24, a student at the Sorbonne and son of a former United States ambassador to Poland, was coming home. Herman Doehner, 50, was en route with his wife and four children to Mexico where he owned a drug firm.

The *Hindenburg* had been due at Lakehurst the morning of May 6, but headwinds prolonged the flight. The airship's passengers had a chance to get an unrivalled view as they passed down the northeast coast. Mr. and Mrs. John Pannes pointed out their home on Long Island, where their son was preparing to leave to meet his parents in Lakehurst.

By 2 P.M. the airship reached New York. After circling the city a few times it moved

**T**he dirigible *Hindenburg* prepares to leave Lakehurst, New Jersey, on a return flight to Germany in the spring of 1935.

on towards Lakehurst. Thunderstorms over New Jersey delayed an afternoon landing, however, and it was not until 7 P.M. that Commander Rosendahl at Lakehurst radioed Captain Pruss that the dirigible could land.

There was a faint drizzle when the *Hindenburg* approached the field. Waiting were 92 sailors and civilians of the ground crew. (The civilians got $1 for the job, but most came out for the excitement. It was like watering the elephant at the circus in the old days.)

The Belins were there to welcome their son; so were Mrs. Spah and her children, the Mangones, the curious, and several newsmen, some veterans of other landings. Associated Press Photographer Murray Becker was there, too, about to take pictures that would become classics.

Near the mooring tower, the ship's crewmen threw down lines. It was 7:20 P.M. Lieutenant Raymond Tyler, chief mooring officer at the naval station, remembers dust rising from the coils as they hit the wet ground.

No one is sure who saw it first.

Perhaps it was two crewmen inside the ship who heard a dull explosion and looked up to see a bright flash in the No. 4 gas cell near the tail. A woman thought the flash she saw was the setting sun finally breaking through the clouds.

"What is it?" said Captain Pruss in the control room. He thought a landing line had snapped. To others, further away, the sound was much louder. Many in the ship heard nothing and one passenger taking pictures of the ground crew wondered why everyone suddenly was rushing.

As soon as he saw the flames, Commander Rosendahl said later, he knew. "It spelled the doom of the ship."

Photographer Becker was hoping to get a shot of the giant airship at the exact moment it made contact with the mooring mast.

"As I stood waiting for the zeppelin to swing around," he said, "a tongue of flame suddenly burst from the tail section. In the next second, the tail section exploded.

"'Oh, my God!' I shouted. I was stunned, but I caught the ship on an even keel before it crashed to the ground seconds later. I was conscious of a terrific blast of heat and of people screaming about me, but

Photo by Murray Becker, Associated Press

Nosing toward its mooring post, the *Hindenburg* bursts into flame as spectators look on in horror.

Photo above © New York Daily News. Photo right by Murray Becker, Associated Press.

These spectacular shots show the *Hindenburg* exploding and being engulfed in flames moments before it touched down.

I ran forward, snapping pictures until the heat drove me back."

Becker carried his film to a nearby hangar.

"Then I just sat down on the ground outside the hangar with my back against the wall and cried. . . . Never had I seen such sudden, stark tragedy."

But Becker's unforgettable photographs didn't catch the terror in the passenger cabin when the nose of the ship lurched upward, when the bust of Hindenburg tumbled from its pedestal in the midst of the falling passengers, when Spah hung from a railing high about the ground, when Mrs. Doehner saved two of her children by throwing them out a window and when Pannes walked away from a window to look for his wife.

Thirteen passengers died, including the Panneses. So did 22 of the 61-man crew and one of the ground crew. But some lived, miraculously.

Miss Mather reached the boarding ramp just as the flames began to eat through its supports. She walked down it onto the ground with hardly a burn. A 14-year-old cabin boy saw burning wreckage about to fall on him when one of the water ballast tanks let go, drenching him—and saving his life.

Captain Pruss escaped, then ran back to help his crewmates. He was badly burned. Captain Lehmann, seared over much of his body, staggered away from the burning wreckage mumbling, "I don't understand, I don't understand."

Passenger O'Laughlin, who had survived an airplane crash the year before, said of the *Hindenburg*: "I never flew in a craft that travelled through the air as easily. Even in breaking up, *Hindenburg* was gentle to its passengers—those that lived."

When he first heard the news, the great German dirigible pioneer Hugo Eckener said, "It must be sabotage." So did Captain Lehmann, just before he died of his burns a short time later.

The U.S. Commerce Department, after lengthy hearings, said most probably it was static electricity that touched off some leaking hydrogen gas. The real cause, however, would never be determined.

But when the *Hindenburg* crashed in flames, it also became the funeral pyre for a romantic, noble era of flight.

Just two days after the stricken airship went to its doom, a German seaplane left the Azores to pioneer a commercial plane route across the North Atlantic, a harbinger of a new age.

**A**lone survivor, lower right, dashes from the inferno of twisted steel that had once been the pride of the German air fleet. Several rescuers rushed forward to pull other passengers and crew members to safety.

**A** sentry stood watch beside the ruins of the *Hindenburg* the morning after. Only a tangled maze of metal remained.

**N**ames of survivors of the *Hindenburg* disaster are posted on the bulletin board at the Lakehurst Naval Station as soon as they are learned. But 36 would die, including 13 passengers, 22 crewmen and one ground crewman.

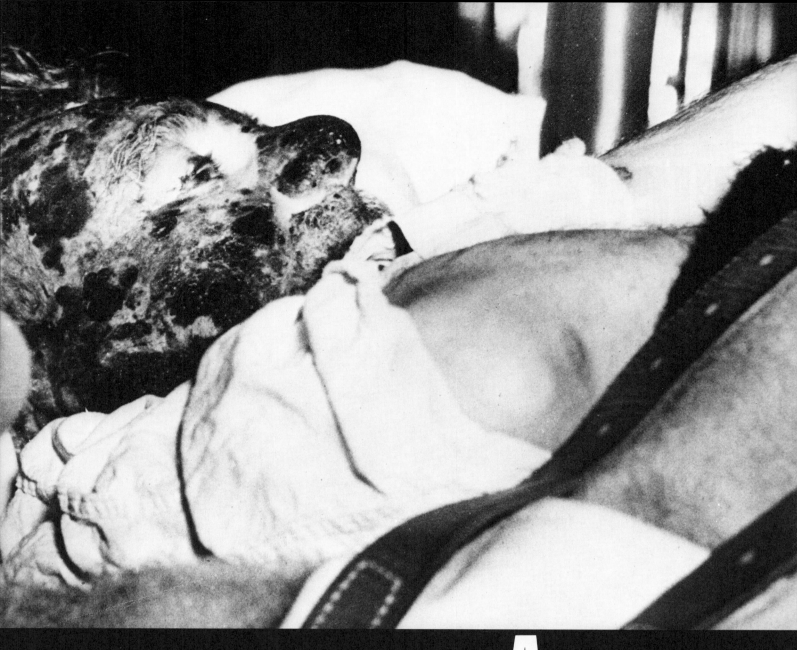

Among the *Hindenburg* survivors was Major Hans Hugo Witt, who was horribly burned.

Services for 28 German nationals who lost their lives in the *Hindenburg* tragedy are held on the Hamburg-American pier before the caskets are loaded aboard a ship for return to Europe. The services are conducted by the German-American Bund, a Nazi organization.

# A NIGHT TO FORGET

**S**moke pours from the Cocoanut Grove Night Club, where a night of revelry turned into a nightmare of death and panic in Boston's Back Bay area. Accidentally started fire claimed 492 lives.

America had been in World War II less than a year and news from the front remained grim. But the 1,000 or so people who crowded into the Cocoanut Grove Club on Boston's Piedmont Street the night of Saturday, November 28, 1942, were there to have a good time, to leave memories of the war behind them for a few hours.

Among the revellers were a number of servicemen and post-game football party-goers.

Shortly after 10:00 P.M., the orchestra leader raised his baton to signal for the national anthem as a prelude to the floor show.

Suddenly, there was a puff of smoke in the darkened club, and a thin finger of flame started to race among the decorations. Someone cried "Fire," and within seconds, pandemonium erupted among the patrons.

What started out as an evening of revelry and relaxation turned out to be the worst nightclub holocaust in the nation's history: 492 dead and hundreds more injured. Some of the victims were so terribly burned that final identification was never possible.

The walls and ceiling of the Cocoanut Grove were hung with colored cloth, and in the main lounge, several poles were topped with artificial palm leaves made of paper and clusters of imitation coconuts.

A 16-year-old busboy, attempting to replace a bulb in a ceiling light, lit a match to see better and accidentally set one of the artificial palm fronds ablaze. A fire alarm was sounded shortly after 10:15. Three additional alarms followed in rapid succession, but long before they had been answered, the dead and injured were piling up inside the club—victims of burns, of smoke inhalation, of their own panic.

Billy Payne, a singer at the club, said he was getting ready to start the show "when I suddenly heard screams. I thought there was a fight. Then I saw a flame racing along the wall. Screams started getting louder and everyone started rushing."

As Payne led a group of 10 people to safety by taking refuge in a huge basement refrigerator room, there was a stampede of screaming patrons headed for the doors of the club.

Bodies later were found piled up at a revolving door, where those seeking a way out were jammed together in the panic and chaos. One door was designed to open inward, another was locked shut. In fact, all of the exits had something wrong with them.

Some of those who escaped made their way to the roof of the building and leaped to the roofs of parked cars below, then to the street. The clothing of some was burning as they fled the club.

Survivors told horror-filled stories of tangled bodies and of men and women tearing the clothes from each other in their panic to escape the searing flames.

William Ladd of Boston said the sudden flash of flame and rolling cloud of smoke touched off an instant panic.

"Men and women began to scream together," he said. "It seemed everyone wanted to get out first. They all got to a small door on Piedmont Street and one of the women went down. Then the other men and women fell on top of her and the bodies just seemed to keep piling up.

"While these people were trapped and tangled with one another, the flames reached the front door. It was impossible then for anyone to get out."

Wilbur Sheffield, an engineer from Newton, Massachusetts, possibly the last person to enter the club, said he was met by a surging crowd. Women's dresses were in flames, he said, and behind the pushing scrambling throng was a sea of fire.

He said he managed to get to the front of the clubroom—only to find a door jammed with others. He finally was able to break through to safety.

Scenes of horror also were witnessed outside the night spot.

Benjamin Ellis had been shopping at a nearby store when he heard someone yell, "There's a fire at the Cocoanut Grove!"

"When I got there," Ellis related, "10 or 15 people were struggling in the doorway. They were men and women. Some were sailors. Their faces were quickly blackened. The smoke was pouring out around them and over their heads.

"In a matter of seconds, a belch of flame came right out. The clothing of the people in the doorway was burning on them. Windows were kicked out and people were hanging out screaming. It was the most terrible thing I have ever seen."

Fire department officials told of body-clogged exitways, which first had to be cleared of victims before the fire fighters could get inside to get at the blaze.

Bartender John W. Bradley, his head swathed in bandages and apparently near collapse with grief, testified two days later:

"There was a flash. Fire ran right across the ceiling. It was awful. I got out through the kitchen. Smoke hit me in the face. I put my hands to my head and my hair was ablaze."

The inferno claimed the lives of 484 patrons—including more than 50 servicemen—and employees. Several others, including motion picture cowboy star Charles (Buck) Jones, were to die of their injuries later. The final toll was 492 dead and 166 injured.

District Fire Chief William J. Mahoney said he had found bodies tangled and piled four or five deep, most of them frightfully burned. He said there was definite evidence that the crowd had been thrown into a fighting, clawing panic. Chairs and tables were tipped and scattered among the bodies.

The dead and injured from Cocoanut Grove fire are laid out on Boston's Piedmont Street waiting removal either to the hospital or morgue. Panic prevented escape for many after fire was first discovered.

Friends and relatives try to identify some of the dead in Cocoanut Grove fire, while ambulance crews check for signs of life among victims.

Boston police and firemen climb through rear windows and entrances of Cocoanut Grove Club in an effort to recover the dead and injured in the disastrous fire.

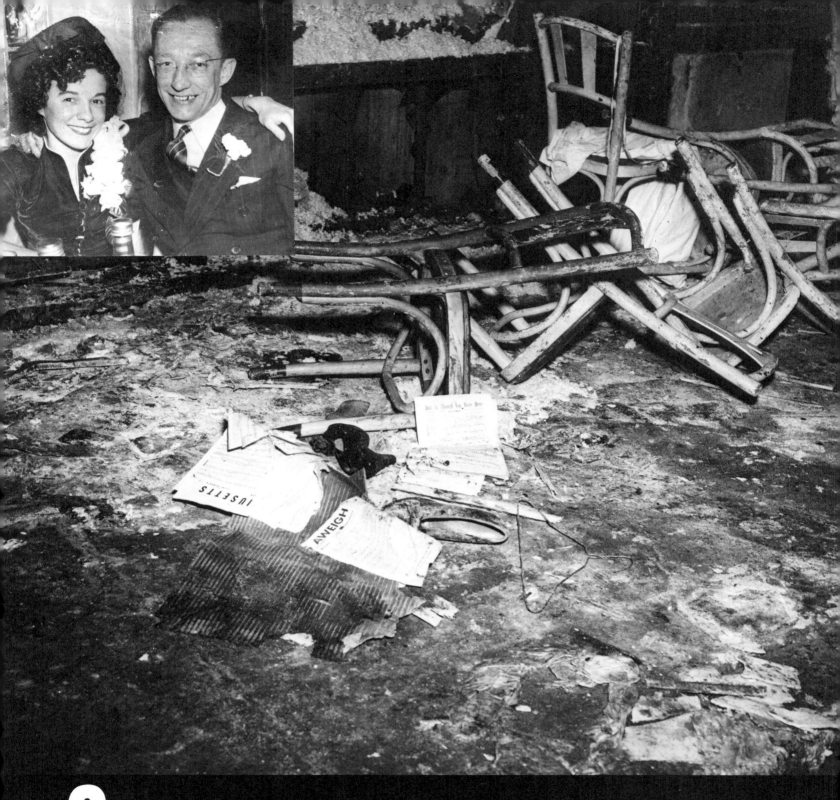

**O**verturned chairs, sheet music and women's shoes remained as mute evidence of the panic which swept the Cocoanut Grove. A night of fun had ended in ashes. *Inset:* Mr. and Mrs. John H. O'Neil of Cambridge, Massachusetts, were celebrating their wedding night and posed for the Cocoanut Grove photographer. A short time later, bride and groom were dead. Somehow the film survived the fire.

As the proportions of the disaster grew, aid was summoned from surrounding cities and towns. Ambulances, beach wagons, private cars, even express trucks with police riding the running boards, were pressed into service to carry the dead and injured to morgues and hospitals.

Hospitals throughout the Boston area were jammed with the injured as blood plasma and sulfa drugs were rushed to Boston from as far away as Washington, D.C. A number of burn specialists were flown in from other cities.

Every medical examiner in the state was called to duty. Soldiers, sailors, Coast Guardsmen and Marines helped carry out the victims even as firemen continued to fight foot by foot through the flames.

Automobiles were shifted from their parking spots near the club to make room for blanket-covered forms, twisted and blackened, some with shoes or other articles of clothing missing.

In the city's two morgues, the gruesome task of trying to identify the dead had begun. Long lines of relatives and friends formed outside the morgues as they waited to be led, two-by-two, past the long rows of bodies, many burned beyond recognition.

By daybreak, all the bodies had been removed from the one-and-a-half-story stucco structure on the narrow Back Bay street.

To some passersby, perhaps, it would have the appearance of a huge brick oven—filled inside with burned and charred wreckage, but with hardly a scorched spot on the outside walls and roof.

But the street, littered with cups, saucers and small wooden cocktail forks that had been washed out by fire hoses the night before, gave mute testimony to the tragedy.

In the aftermath of the fire, indictments were brought against the owner of the Cocoanut Grove and its management. Members of various city departments who were responsible for public safety were also brought to trial for laxity, incompetence and failure to fulfill their prescribed duties.

The owner, Barney Welansky, was sentenced to 10 to 15 years in state prison. He served three years and seven months. All others were cleared or given suspended sentences.

The disaster also brought attention to inadequate fire-safety requirements in public buildings. Cities all across the nation revised their building and fire codes from what had been learned from Cocoanut Grove.

**T**his dramatic photograph shows a Boston priest administering last rites to a woman dragged from the fire-swept Cocoanut Grove Club.

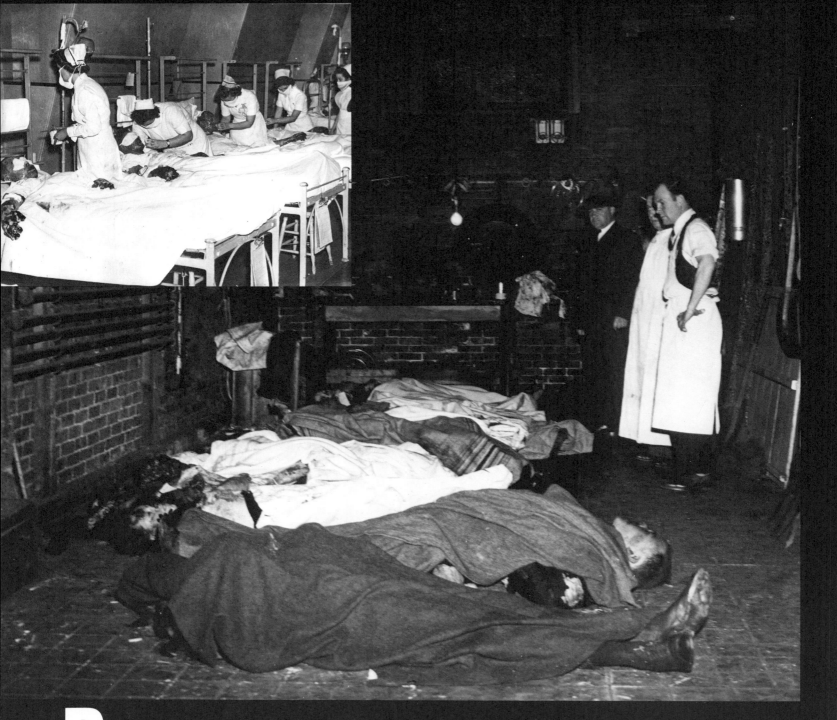

**B**odies of some of the scores of dead from the fire which swept the Cocoanut Grove were taken to this Boston mortuary to await identification. *Inset:* Several severely burned victims are attended by nurses at Boston City Hospital. Many would succumb to their injuries, including cowboy film star Charles (Buck) Jones.

On the morning after the Cocoanut Grove fire, a charred and blistered front entrance gives grim evidence to the deadly blaze that swept the nightclub the evening before.

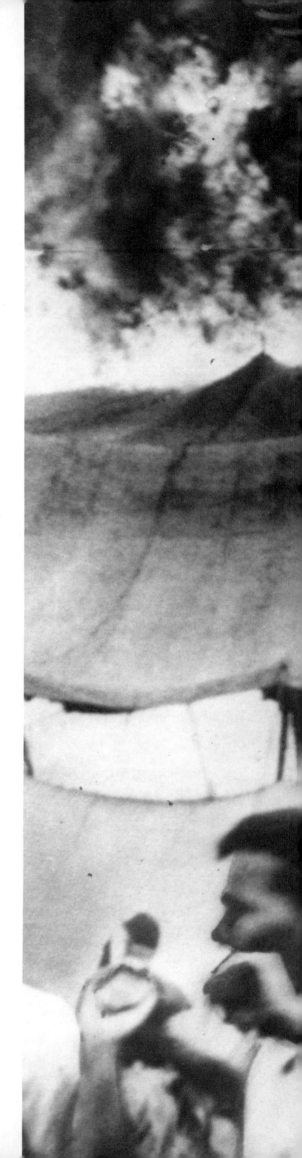

# A DAY AT THE CIRCUS

**D**eath joined the act when fire raced through the Big Top in Hartford, Connecticut. In 20 minutes, 168 circusgoers lay dead and more than 500 were injured. *Inset:* Merle Evans, leader of the Ringling Bros. band, before tragedy interrupted his performance.

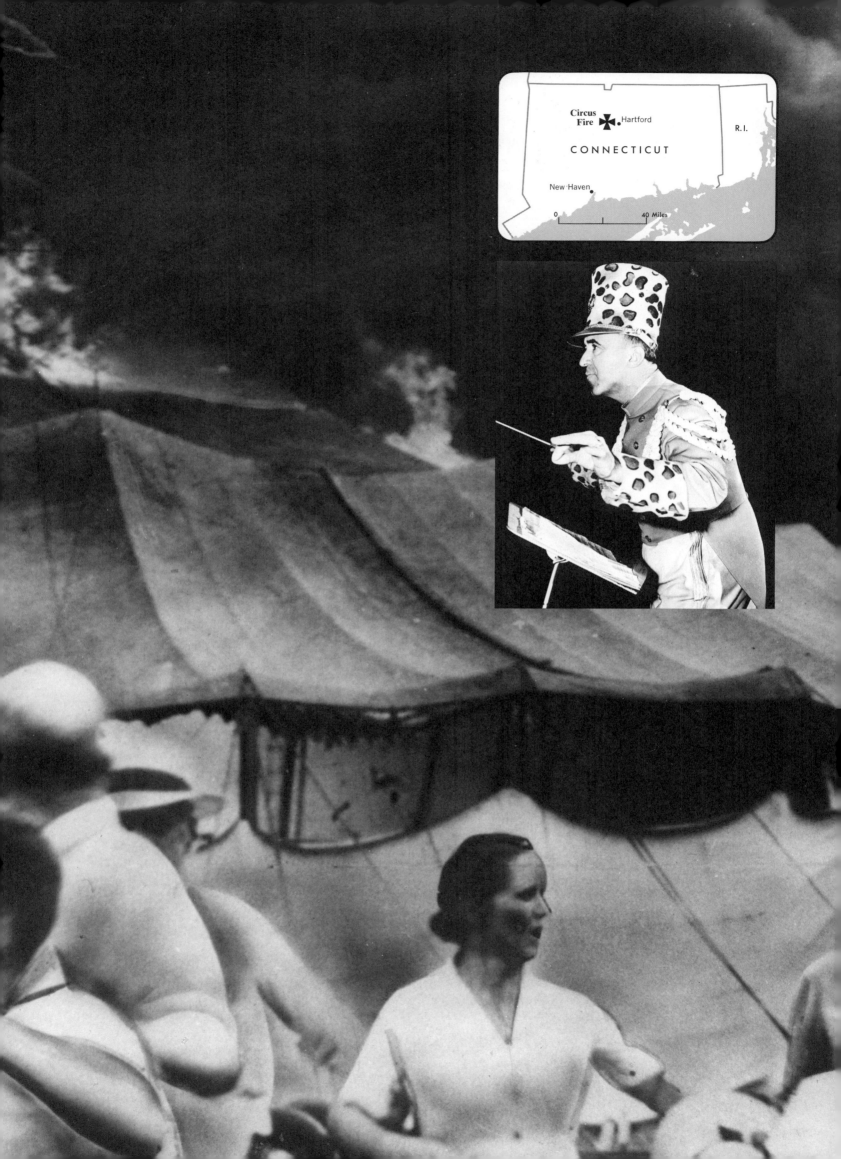

Circus
Fire ✠ Hartford

CONNECTICUT

R. I.

New Haven

0          40 Miles

July 6, 1944, dawned hot and humid in Hartford, Connecticut. Ringling Bros. and Barnum & Bailey Circus was in town for a one-day stand.

Just before the matinee started, a 6-year-old girl with curly brown hair took her seat under the big top along with some 6,000 other men, women and children.

The atmosphere inside the huge tent was gay, laughing and excited.

At 2 P.M., Merle Evans, veteran bandmaster for the circus, led his 29-piece band through a snappy opening number. Then came the clowns, acrobats and animals.

At 2:40, Evans spotted a small, horse-shoe-shaped tongue of flame creeping up the side of the main tent, just as the Wallendas, a famed high-wire troupe, reached their perch above the crowd.

Suddenly, Evans switched the band from ballet music—the exit tune for the animal act—to a stirring march, "The Stars and Stripes Forever." For the circus-wise, the abrupt change was the dreaded warning that danger lurked in the big top. Later, Evans explained it could have been any other snappy tune, but he picked Sousa's famed march because it was familiar and might avoid a panic.

Momentarily, the flame looked small enough to extinguish with a bucket of water. But within seconds, the flames, sparked by stiff winds, grew into a roaring, horrifying caldron. And by 3 P.M., the flaming envelope which had engulfed 6,000 spectators was a smouldering bier. The little girl with the brown curls was among the 168 people who perished in the fire and ensuing panic. More than 500 others were injured.

More than 1,000 circus animals, including 40 lions, an equal number of elephants, tigers, leopards, and other beasts were out of harm's way.

Thomas E. Murphy, an editorial writer for the *Hartford Courant,* was attending the circus that day with his 5-year-old son.

"The Wallendas had just climbed up the rope ladder to their perch when I heard a woman gasp behind me, 'Look, fire!' There, near the main entrance to the tent, a tiny tongue of flame crept up the side wall.

"Almost automatically the people rose to their feet. Several men shouted, 'Take it easy. Take it easy. Walk out quietly.'

"The crowd seemed to subside for an instant. But then, with almost unbelievable speed, the tiny flame spread into a devouring curtain of fire that rushed toward the top. All semblance of order was gone. Now women screamed, children cried.

On the circus grounds, only charred bleachers remained from the worst circus fire in history.

"I saw one woman in the top row take her flaxen-haired little girl in one arm, grab a rope in the other and slide to the ground. Her arm was red and raw.

"Running from the animal cages in the back to the exhibition cages were two steel runways three feet high. These were still in place, and as the crowd surged forward, people had to climb over this steel barrier. I saw one woman fail to make it, slide back and slump to the ground. A man tried to fend the crowd back from her, but the pressure was too great.

"I was slammed against the steel barrier and my knee caught momentarily between the bars. Then, taking my 5-year-old son in my hands, I tossed him over the barrier to the ground beyond. The flames at this point were nearly overhead and the heat was becoming unbearable.

"I looked back over my shoulder as I left the tent and saw people still struggling madly to get over the barrier. Outside, children were running around crying. Men and women had that vacant look of shock. Some were sitting on the grass just staring into space."

Clarence E. Wilson was about to depart the circus grounds after leaving his wife and child at the big tent when he spotted the burst of flame. He said the tent went up "in a puff of smoke" and within 10 minutes it lay like a sheet of burned paper.

"I saw rows of charred bodies, lying between the burned bleachers. They showed no evidence of being trampled on, but were just scorched and burned. The heat was intense and women and children were running out of the grounds. Men were crying for their children. There was a terrible howling and screeching and panic." It was only later that Wilson learned that his wife and son had escaped to safety.

Other eyewitnesses said that many were killed and injured in the rush for the exits. The fire never touched the victims.

For Shirley Snelgrove, a trip to the circus was part of her 13th birthday celebration.

"We were having a birthday party—mother, father and I," Shirley said. "The fire started opposite us—I saw it right away—and the three of us went to the top of the bleachers. But we lost our nerve to jump and thought we'd try to get to the main entrance.

"Mother and father went across the animal cages, but I couldn't get across them. Then I got separated from my parents and went back to the top of the bleachers. I jumped then."

Badly burned, Shirley was dragged

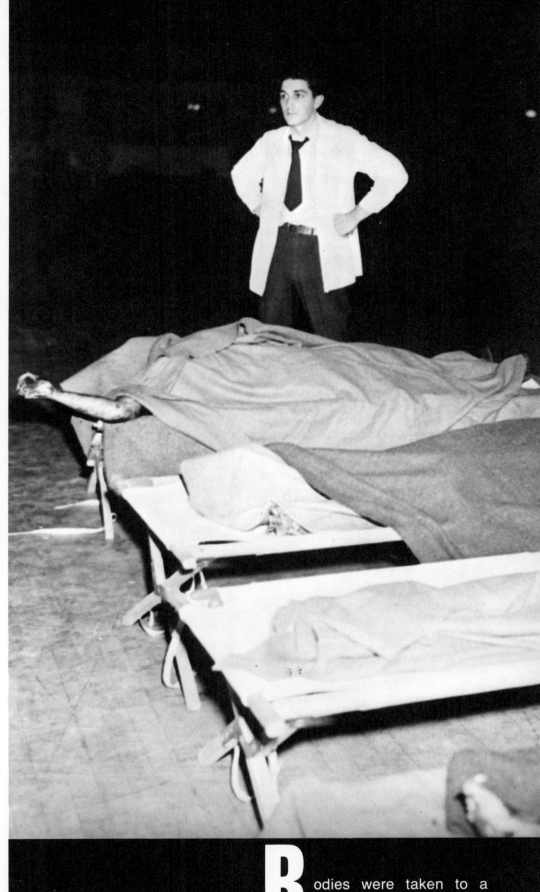

**W**orkers and firemen view the charred remains of several of the victims. What started as a day of gaiety for them ended as a fiery nightmare.

**B**odies were taken to a nearby armory where the grim task of identifying many of the victims was begun. Some never were identified.

from under the flaming tent. Her parents died in the fire.

Scores of men, women and children tried with varying success to jump from high seats. Many children were dropped bodily from the top levels of the bleachers to make their way as best they could to safety. At least two-thirds of the dead were children.

"Their cries," said an eyewitness, "were awful to hear." For many of those children, there was no escape as the flames overtook them.

As the injured were sped to hospitals all over Hartford, the dead were removed to an armory. That night, thousands of persons made their way through row upon row of blanket-covered cots to try to identify the victims, many of whom were burned beyond recognition.

The cause of the fire was never definitely established. The explanation most generally accepted is that it was started by a cigarette carelessly tossed into a canvas men's room just outside the main entrance of the big tent. But out of the fire emerged mountains of financial and legal troubles for the circus.

Six circus officials eventually were charged with involuntary manslaughter. They were accused by a coroner's official finding of being guilty of "wanton or reckless conduct, either of commission or of omission where there is a duty to act." They pleaded no contest and received jail terms.

For days following the fire, Hartford was stunned, full of heartache. And at least one sorrow has remained with the city down through the years—the mystery of the 6-year-old girl with the brown curly hair.

Though the flames left her pretty face virtually unmarred, she was never identified. They still call her "Little Miss 1565." The name she has borne in death was taken from a numbered casualty tag placed on her body when it was brought into a temporary morgue following the holocaust.

On the first anniversary of the tragedy, two Hartford policemen who participated in the mammoth task of identifying the dead placed flowers on her grave in Northwood Cemetery in nearby Windsor. And for years, Lieutenant Thomas C. Barber and Sergeant Edward T. Lowe repeated the ceremony on the fire anniversary, Memorial Day and Christmas Eve.

"It just doesn't seem possible," one of the policemen said, "that a child like that little one could have disappeared from her own small world without somebody noticing that she had gone and never came back."

**J**oint services were held at a mass burial of several of the victims of the circus fire, with policemen serving as pallbearers.

# FROM OUT OF THE FOG

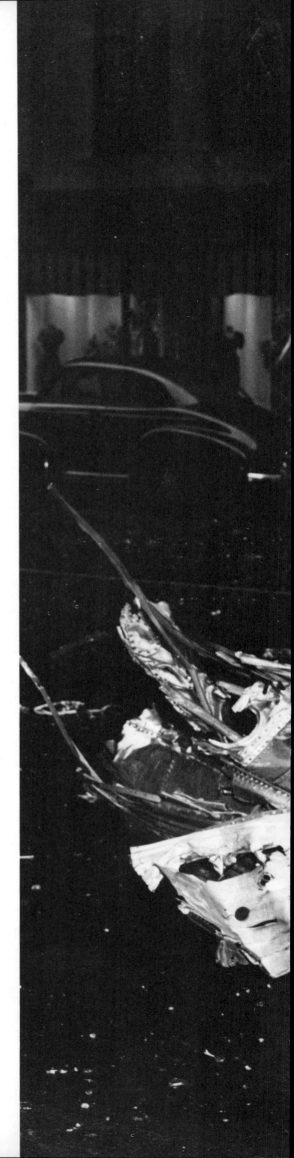

**M**ilitary officer examines a portion of wreckage of ill-fated Army bomber which crashed into Empire State Building. This large piece fell on 34th Street, a busy New York City thoroughfare. *Inset:* Key areas involved in the bomber crash are located in this view looking south.

102nd Floor

Observation Platform

86th Floor

MAIN AREA OF FIRE

913 Feet To Street

79th Floor

PLANE HIT IN THIS AREA

72nd Floor

Fifth Avenue

34th Street

W. 42 ST. E.

Grand Central Station

Broadway

New York Public Library

Seventh Ave.

Park Ave.

W. 34 ST.

B-25 Crash

Empire State Building

Pennsylvania Station

Fifth Ave.

W. 30 ST.

0

¼ Mile

**T**he B-25, groping its way through fog, rammed into the 79th floor of the Empire State Building.

She was born in the Depression and saw hard times in her youth. The Empire State Building, then the tallest structure ever built by man, was formally opened May 1, 1931, when President Herbert Hoover pressed a button in Washington to turn on the lights on New York's Fifth Avenue between 33rd and 34th Streets.

Her vital statistics were mighty impressive: more than a quarter-of-a-mile high (102 stories), enough steel to build a railroad from New York to Baltimore, seven miles of elevator shaft and an 80-mile view into four states on a clear day.

But it wasn't a clear day on Saturday, July 28, 1945, when this majestic building became a casualty of World War II.

An Army B-25, on a cross-country mission which started in Bedford, Massachusetts, was groping its way through heavy fog toward the Newark, New Jersey, airport, when it rammed into the 79th floor of the skyscraper—913 feet above Manhattan—and brought flaming death to 14 people. Three of those killed were aboard the plane; the others were workers trapped in their offices. Twenty-six others were injured.

The Billy Mitchell bomber, piloted by Lieutenant Colonel William F. Smith, 27, of Watertown, Massachusetts, struck the building shortly before 10 A.M., shaking the area like an earthquake and sending blazing gasoline cascading through offices and down elevator shafts. Colonel Smith, a crewman and a passenger died.

Only moments before the crash, the pilot had communicated with LaGuardia Airport by radio and was told by the control tower that not even the top of the Empire State Building could be seen because of the fog. The plane continued southward down Fifth Avenue at a dangerously low altitude

and then struck the tower-spiked structure.

The point of greatest impact was at the offices of the National Catholic Welfare Conference, where many of the fatalities occurred—mostly women stenographers caught beneath toppled or crushed partitions.

Fifteen hundred persons were in the building at the time of the crash. On a normal midweek business day, the building's population is 15,000.

Three explosions were heard as the plane sheared through the stone exterior of the structure, which, some witnesses said, swayed like a tree in the wind. Flaming gasoline spread through offices and corridors, and the screams of the trapped, many badly burned, spread panic in the upper stories.

Great chunks of debris were hurled from the flame-and-smoked-wrapped tower for five blocks around. One flaming engine blasted through the south wall of the building and fell atop a 12-story building a block away and set the roof afire. It was put out minutes later.

One of the most hair-raising experiences was recounted from a hospital bed by 20-year-old Betty Lou Oliver of Fort Smith, Arkansas, who was working as an elevator operator in the building while she waited in New York for her sailor husband to return from overseas.

Mrs. Oliver, who had given notice and planned to quit in a few days, was alone in the car when its cables were severed by portions of the bomber. She fell nearly 1,000 feet, from the 79th floor to the sub-basement.

"The elevator seemed to stop and shudder for a moment," she said. "Then it began plummeting downward. I tried desperately to stop it. Then a flash of fire covered me and I raised my left arm to protect my face.

"The fire was gone in a moment and I tried again to work the controls. I picked up the telephone in the cage and tried to call the starter on the ground floor. Nothing happened. I started yelling and pounding the floor. I felt as though the car were leaving me. I was going down so fast that I just had to hang onto the sides to keep from floating."

The elevator crashed against an oil buffer in the bottom of the pit, driving the buffer through the car and smashing the floor—all except for a few square inches on which Mrs. Oliver stood. She suffered severe burns and bruises, but survived.

Outside, fire trucks and ambulances converged on the scene as thousands of spectators gathered in the streets. Mounted policemen and patrol cars parked bumper to bumper kept the crowds from inching any closer to the disaster area.

Firemen entering the Catholic Welfare Conference suite on the 79th floor saw a grisly sight—nine charred bodies grouped around a single table. Another body was found further back on the same floor.

Still another was found on the parapet of the 72nd floor. It was that of Paul Dearing, publicity man for the Catholic organization and a former Buffalo, New York, reporter. Police said the crash apparently threw him from his office and out of the building to the wing roof six stories below.

There were several eyewitness accounts of the actual crash.

Frank E. Sieverman III, a department store executive, said he was sitting in his office in a nearby building "when the plane crashed near the top of the building with a stunning roar. The plane was obviously out of control and flying extremely low. As it neared the building, the pilot seemed to try

New York City's towering Empire State Building becomes a beacon of death for an Army bomber headed for Newark, New Jersey. This overhead view looks down on the gaping hole in the side of the building above 34th Street.

and veer away, but it struck squarely."

And sports announcer Stan Lomax was in his automobile stopped for a light nearby when, he said, the plane flew straight down Fifth Avenue and into the building.

"There was the damnedest ball of fire you ever saw. It was a tremendous big burst of flame. A wing of the plane shot down to the left toward Madison Avenue. The remainder of the plane stuck right in the building. It was an inferno."

Fifty people were in the observation tower at the time, but they were removed from the building—along with hundreds of others—without incident.

But there were narrow escapes for some.

Daniel Norden, employed in an 80th floor office, said he, another man and an hysterical woman were trapped by flames at the door and windows. He said they were able to escape by knocking a hole in one wall with a carpenter's hammer.

Philip Kerby, working in an advertising agency on the 76th floor, told of preventing a woman from jumping out a window when flaming gasoline poured into her office.

Among the grieving families who assembled at the city morgue the following day to help identify the victims was Charles Bath, whose 19-year-old wife, Lucille, was listed as missing.

"If only she didn't go in yesterday—it was her vacation—she would be alive now. I pleaded with her to stay home and go to the beach with me. She didn't have to go in."

Mrs. Bath was a clerk for the war relief service of the Catholic agency.

But perhaps the saddest of all the stories told was that concerning 19-year-old Naval Machinist Albert G. Penna of Brooklyn, New York, who had hitched-hiked a ride to death aboard the Army bomber.

He was en route to his parents, who were already grief-stricken over the death of their only other son a few weeks before in the Pacific. That son had lost his life when his destroyer was sunk.

"We insisted that Albert not travel by plane," the father said. "Just the week before, he came home by plane and it frightened his mother. Albert promised us he wouldn't go on another plane. He promised. We wanted him home because he was the only one who could comfort his mother."

Ironically, less than 24 hours before the crash, federal officials had met with engineers to discuss the possible development of anti-collision equipment, operating as a radio beacon, atop the 102-story building. Had such a device been in operation, it might have averted the tragedy.

Mayor Fiorello LaGuardia, who had long campaigned against planes flying at low altitude over Manhattan's skyscrapers, said the bomber crash was "one of those accidents which are the more regrettable because they are avoidable."

Damage to the building was estimated at $500,000, relatively light considering the type of disaster which occurred. But claims against the Army as a result of the crash amounted to more than $3 million, mostly from survivors of the victims' families.

Officially, the War Department attributed the accident to unfavorable flying conditions, "misjudgment" on the part of the pilot and partially the fault of the control tower at LaGuardia Airport, which, the Army said, should not have permitted the plane to continue on to Newark because of flying conditions.

Firemen search charred ruins near gaping hole in then world's tallest building. *Inset:* A wheel of the bomber is lodged in the elevator shaft. This view is from the 79th floor looking down the shaft to the floor below.

# DEATH—THE UNINVITED GUEST

T he morning after. Firemen and rescue workers already started moving the dead out of the Winecoff Hotel for identification.

For many years, the Winecoff Hotel stood as a landmark in downtown Atlanta. Built in 1914, the imposing 15-story brick, concrete and steel structure faced Atlanta's famed Peachtree Street just about half a block away from the theater where the world premiere for "Gone With the Wind" was staged.

The Winecoff was considered one of the city's leading hostelries and a major establishment, a first-rate hotel. It also was considered "fire resistant," and had met all safety codes from the day it had first opened its doors for business.

Even 70-year-old W. F. Winecoff, who built the hotel and operated it for 21 years, continued to live in his 10th-floor hotel apartment after he sold the place. It was, indeed, a nice place to stay.

On the night of December 7, 1946, the Winecoff Hotel was packed to capacity with 285 guests filling its 194 rooms. Among the visitors were some 50 boys and girls from all over Georgia who were in Atlanta for a youth conference.

Sometime between 3:15 A.M. and 3:30 A.M., a bellman delivered ice water to a guest's room on the fifth floor. When he left the room a few minutes later, he found himself trapped in the corridor by a wall of smoke and flame.

A fire, at first believed started by a carelessly tossed cigarette in a hallway on the third floor, had already started racing through the "fire resistant" Winecoff Hotel with frightful speed.

The blaze roared out of control within minutes after it was discovered and before fire fighting equipment could be summoned.

By the time it was over, Atlanta would be the site of the worst hotel fire in American history—a conflagration which claimed 119 lives and injured at least 100 more persons.

Horrified onlookers would see men, women and children plunge screaming to their deaths on the pavements below their windows as they sought to escape the searing flames, while scores of others were trapped and burned or suffocated in upstairs rooms.

The sides of the tall, chimney-like structure became draped with torn bed sheets and blankets, marking the rooms where victims tried to escape. Eyewitnesses told how panic-stricken guests swung from 10th and 12th-story windows on flimsy makeshift ropes. A few were rescued, but most fell headlong as flames burned away their supports or they lost their grip.

At one time, half a dozen broken bodies lay at the intersection of Peachtree and Carnegie Way. Onlookers told of seeing many forms silhouetted against boiling flames, praying vainly for succor that could not reach them. Thudding bodies crashed in ghastly procession into the street and smoke-filled alleyways.

Newsman E. J. (Chick) Hosch said he saw many persons leap to their deaths, including one woman who threw her young son and daughter from a seventh-floor window, then followed them to her death too.

"I never expect to hear anything so terrible as the screams of those people from the time they would jump until they struck the pavement," he said.

**HOTEL WINECOFF**

ABSOLUTELY FIREPROOF EUROPEAN PLAN
200 ROOMS EACH WITH INDIVIDUAL BATH

LOCATED NEARER THAN ANYTHING TO EVERYTHING
ON ATLANTA'S MOST FAMOUS THOROUGHFARE
PEACHTREE STREET

**ATLANTA 1, GA.**

L.O.MOSELEY, MANA...

A guest hangs out of an upper-story window as flames erupt from windows just below. Fire hoses could barely reach the upper floors. *Inset:* Ironically, even the hotel stationery promoted the Winecoff Hotel as "absolutely fireproof."

One man was observed trying to reach a fireman's ladder. He swung down from a rope and hung between the building and the ladder. Two other persons jumped or fell from above, struck him, and all three fell to their deaths.

Another reporter saw a man outlined against a panel of fire in an eighth-floor corner window. His clothing caught fire as he waved vainly, and his head rolled helplessly from side to side. Then he fell back out of sight as a huge gush of flame roared from the window.

The flames had spread with disastrous rapidity through the southwest side of the building, racing up an open stairwell and elevator shafts to trap nearly half the guests. Night clerk Comer Rowan said very few guests came downstairs after the alarm sounded and a bell captain reported that racing flames had blocked the stair exits. Elevators had been knocked out almost immediately.

Some who kept their heads were saved. Mrs. Banks Whiteman, manager of the hotel cigar counter, pulled the wife and children of her employer from their 14th-floor apartment, fled to the 15th floor and there huddled in a corner until the fire subsided.

Nelson Thatch, a room clerk who lived on the sixth floor, pleaded with a woman one floor below, but she leaped to her death in an alley. Another woman was restrained from jumping by bell captain William Mobley and an unidentified Army major.

Mr. and Mrs. T. G. Turk of Tulsa, Oklahoma, held their 2-year-old daughter, Nancy Dianne, outside their window until firemen reached them. Turk's two brothers swung from the tenth to the ninth floor on bed sheets and also were rescued.

James Little of Elizabethton, Tennessee, said he pleaded with a friend, but the latter jumped in panic from an eighth-floor window. "I couldn't stop him. If he would have waited five more minutes he would have been saved," said Little.

Mr. and Mrs. M. C. Conners of Montgomery, Alabama, had a hair-raising escape. They were on the 14th floor when Mrs. Conners was awakened by screams. When they found the hallway full of smoke and flames, they put on their coats, climbed out on a window ledge, and edged across a ladder laid down by firemen from an adjoining building. They suffered only slight burns.

But others were not so fortunate.

One of the victims was Patsy Griffin, 14-year-old daughter of Brigadier General Marvin Griffin, adjutant general of Georgia. She was severely burned and later died of her injuries.

Also killed in the disaster was Winecoff, builder of the hotel, who was found in

A woman leaps to her death from one of the upper floors in an effort to escape the searing flames. This photograph, taken by an amateur photographer, was awarded a Pulitzer Prize.

This woman, her head on folded arms, lies dead in a window of the Winecoff Hotel, one of 119 persons whose lives were snuffed out in the Atlanta fire.

his upper floor apartment.

And 28 of the boys and girls who were in Atlanta to take part in the second annual State Youth Assembly of the YMCA also perished.

Mrs. A. R. Minnix of Columbus, Georgia, was crying hysterically when firemen reached her fifth-floor room. She said her 15-year-old son had been trapped on the 11th floor where he was assigned when they were unable to get rooms together. The boy later was listed among the known dead.

In one burned-out room occupied by a youth conference delegate, a Bible was found open at a burial verse.

By 9:00 A.M., Atlanta firemen—25 of whom were overcome by smoke or injured by falling debris—had put out the flames and the grim job of removing the dead was begun. Some victims were so severely burned immediate identification was impossible. Others were huddled dead in their rooms, overcome by the toxic smoke.

Although fire officials blamed the fire initially on a careless cigarette smoker, an insurance investigation later could not substantiate this. The actual cause was never determined, but the report said that the fire had gained considerable headway from the third to fifth floor before its discovery.

Investigators blamed an open stairwell for the rapid spread of the flames. It created a chimney effect, providing a natural draft which spread fire, heated gases and smoke through the upper-floor corridors, cutting off the escape of hotel occupants.

A grand jury later returned involuntary manslaughter indictments against the three operators of the hotel for failure to provide outside fire escapes. These indictments later were dismissed by the Georgia Supreme Court, which held unconstitutional the state's fire escape act of 1910 as "class legislation."

The court had outlawed the act because it required fire escapes on hotels charging two dollars or more per day for rooms, but made no provision for the protection of guests in cheaper hostelries.

But the Winecoff Hotel tragedy did serve as a catalyst for the creation of new hotel safety regulations across the nation, including smoke alarms, sprinkler systems, fire doors and other safety improvements.

Although the interior of the Winecoff Hotel was charred and gutted, the shell of the building remained in relatively good shape. It later was remodeled and was reopened as the Peachtree Hotel.

Several years ago, having already seen its best—and worst—days as a hostelry, the Peachtree was donated to the Georgia Baptist Convention, which now operates the place as a senior citizens home.

Many of the victims were taken to a nearby funeral home for identification (*top*). *Above:* A victim of the fire is carried down a gutted corridor.

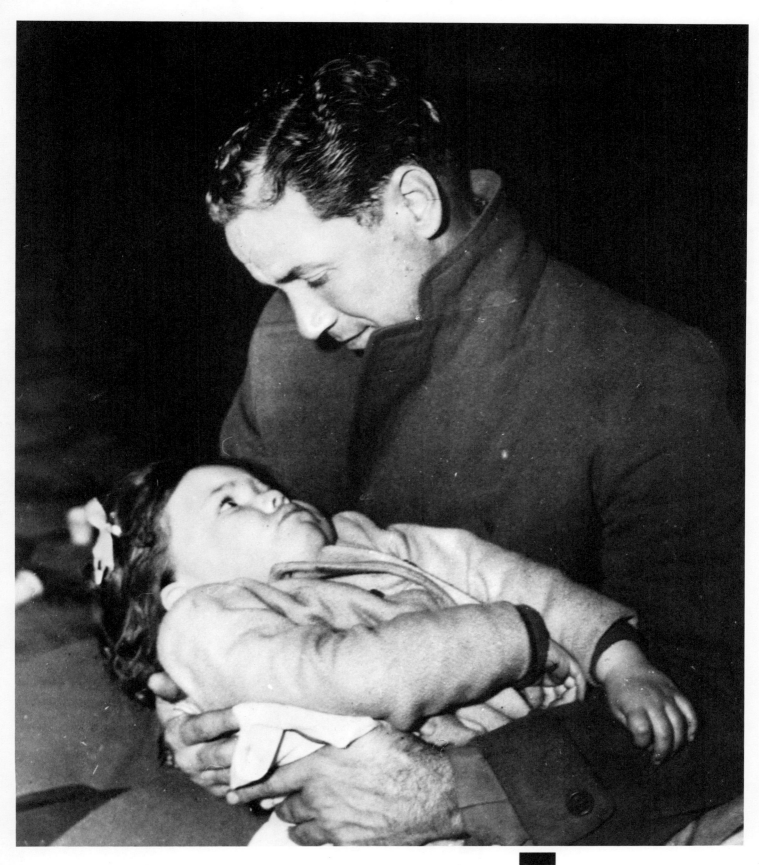

**T**homas Turk held Nancy, his 2-year-old daughter, out of a hotel window for 30 minutes until firemen reached them and carried them down a ladder.

# A CARGO OF DOOM

**A** pall of smoke hangs over the dock area in Texas City, Texas, just after a French freighter, carrying a cargo of ammonium nitrate, blew up in the harbor, leaving 512 dead. *Inset:* An aerial view that resembles World War II bomb devastation is actually the Monsanto Chemical plant five days later.

Houston

*Galveston*
*Bay*

T E X A S

Texas City ✠ **Ship Explosion**

0       20 Miles

•Galveston

On the morning of April 16, 1947, Texas City, Texas, a small but bustling port community on Galveston Bay, almost ceased to exist.

On that morning, a French freighter, carrying a lethal cargo of ammonium nitrate, blew up in the harbor and set off a devastating series of explosions.

Before the pall of smoke had disappeared, one of the worst explosion disasters in United States history had left 512 people dead, more than 3,000 injured, two-thirds of Texas City destroyed and more than $51 million in damages.

The day had started out like most other working days in Texas City. Warehouse and dock workers were loading and unloading berthed oil tankers and ships as other ships slid in and out of the bay. Big oil and chemical plants which dotted the waterfront were alive with activity. Elsewhere in Texas City, children were on their way to school and housewives had begun their chores.

Then, at 8:25, Julien Gueril, a ship's carpenter, discovered a small fire in the No. 4 hold of the freighter *Grandcamp*, which was docked at the waterfront.

Volunteer firemen rushed to the ship, but could not control the fire, which crept closer to the cargo of explosive ammonium nitrate, used in the production of fertilizer. The crew tried to tow the ship away from the dock, but it was too late.

Thirty-seven minutes after the fire was discovered, the *Grandcamp* blew up in an ear-shattering roar. In moments, Texas City was a city of flames, torn steel and smoking rubble.

From the *Grandcamp*, explosions skipped in one-two-three order to the huge Monsanto Chemical Company nearby, then to the Stone Oil Refinery. Giant storage tanks erupted into orange and black waves of flame. Buildings and houses crumbled from the concussion of the blasts and scores of workers were trapped in the wreckage.

Red-hot chunks of steel streamed into the skies from the force of the explosions and showered a wide area of the city. A man driving a car a mile away was killed by a falling fragment. Swirling columns of smoke spread over the city like a giant blanket.

The screams of the dying soon mixed with a chorus of police, fire and ambulance sirens. Heat, smoke, fumes and flames made

rescue work hazardous. For the next 16 hours, fire and additional explosions ravaged the area and continued to heap sorrow and misery on Texas City. The largest blast occurred several hours after the *Grandcamp* explosion when the cargo of ammonium nitrate on another ship, the S.S. *High Flyer*, went off like a giant skyrocket.

A light plane flying over the blast area at the time was blown from the air and its two occupants killed. The force of the explosion tossed a large steel barge across a 25-foot embankment onto dry land.

The blasts shattered windows at Galveston, 11 miles across the bay. The cloud of smoke could be seen from as far away as Houston, a distance of 30 miles.

First witnesses to come into the area after the explosions saw workers streaming from buildings with blood gushing from nose and ears, the result of concussion. A reporter for the *Houston Chronicle* said that bodies "had been tossed about like playing cards."

Philip Flores, a young Army veteran, was working 25 yards from the *Grandcamp*.

"The concussion knocked me down," he said. "I crawled over to some flour sacks and buried my head under them. Then a few seconds later the [Monsanto] chemical plant exploded. The roof and walls of the warehouse were coming down around me. I got up and ran for my life.

"Later, I helped pull bodies out of the wreckage. It was the most terrible thing I've seen. One man with a leg blown off was screaming in pain. I could not tell you how he looked because he did not have much face left. Most of the bodies were mangled."

Associated Press newsman Bill Barnard arrived in Texas City the night of April 16 and described the scene:

"This is a city where the dead are uncounted and the living are too dazed and weary to cry.

"Tonight scores of explosion and fire dead are stacked on benches and tables in a large midtown garage and in the nearby high school gymnasium. Outside these places the people gather in silent, expressionless groups. Dozens of embalmers were brought in and there the slow process of identification goes on.

"A mile away, black smoke from six roaring fires billows 5,000 feet into the air

The thick, dense smoke from a burning oil refinery provides the backdrop for a home shattered in the blast. The explosions destroyed about two-thirds of the Texas port city.

and drifts southward out over the Gulf. A 50-acre area of devastation marks the scene where the explosions of two ships and a chemical works wrought the greatest tragedy this area has ever known. . . .

"I stood in the City Hall and saw a woman find the name of her son on a casualty list. Her shoulders sagged, her arms fell limp at her sides and her face twisted with grief. Her husband, his face a glazed mask, caught her under the arm and led her out.

"I went to the scene of the *Grandcamp* explosion. There was no ship left. Only kindling floated on dark, oily water."

Just before night fell, a group of priests from Houston probed deep into the smoke and wreckage with flashlights to try to administer last sacraments to the dead still in the debris.

"It is an indescribable tragedy," said Father M. A. Record. "I saw charred bodies being brought out—and I even saw them floating in the water."

W. H. Sanberg, a vice-president of the Texas City Terminal Railway Co., said he had been on the *Grandcamp* five minutes before it blew up, but left to return to his office nearby to make emergency telephone calls in connection with the fire.

Although he was severely cut, Sanberg was able to save his life by taking refuge under his rolltop desk.

He described the concussion as "simply terrible. It blew out windows of every home in town. It blew in ceilings of business buildings. It cracked new buildings from end to end. Doors were blown from their hinges."

Several hundred curious were on the docks to watch the firefighters battle the blaze aboard the *Grandcamp*. When the ship blew up, scores of onlookers perished.

At the Monsanto plant, 227 of its employees and construction workers died in the explosion and ensuing fires.

The people of Texas City were stunned. There was hardly a person who didn't have a relative or friend on the casualty list.

But long before all the bodies were recovered from the debris, Texas City was mapping plans for the future and, within a decade, all visible scars of the devastation had disappeared.

After the disaster, federal court suits seeking more than $200 million in damages from the United States government were filed by property owners, those injured in the disaster and the relatives of the dead. They argued that the government was responsible in that the nitrate was produced in government-owned ordnance plants.

The Supreme Court ruled, however, that the government was not negligent, and it took an act of Congress to authorize a maximum award of $75,000 to each Texas City claim approved by the Secretary of the Army. Eventually, the federal government was to pay more than $16 million in claims for death, personal injury and property losses.

The final claim was paid 10 years after the disaster—but far from the scene where it occurred.

Mme. Ann M. Thirion of Finistère, France, whose husband, Jean, was killed aboard the *Grandcamp*, received a check for $25,000.

This victim, his arms and legs dangling horribly, lies mangled in the wreckage of a waterfront plant devastated in the blast.

Four dazed and battered rescue workers limp back from the danger area along the Texas City waterfront shortly after a new series of explosions and fires swept the area.

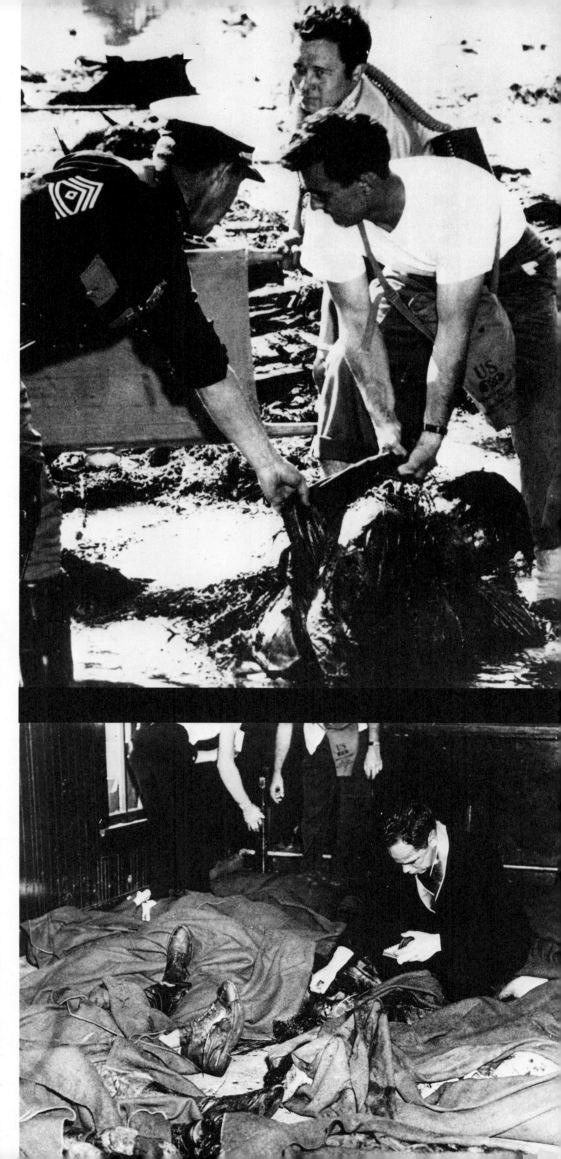

**A**n unidentified couple loads household goods and personal effects onto a battered pickup truck as they prepare to leave their home in the fire-blackened city.

**B**ut others were not so lucky. Here rescuers dig a body out of a mud flat where the victim was hurled by the force of the blast.

**O**ther dead were taken to a temporary morgue set up near the explosion scene. In this grim photograph, a priest administers last rites to one of a number of victims of the deadly blast.

# PRIDE OF THE GREAT LAKES

**T**he still-smouldering *Noronic* lies in Toronto Harbor after a nighttime blaze reduced her to a gutted hulk. It was called the worst Great Lakes disaster in more than a century.

The S.S. *Noronic,* largest pleasure ship traveling the waters of the Great Lakes, sat comfortably moored at Queen's Quay in Toronto Harbor.

She was a magnificent sight. She was well illuminated along her 362 feet from bow to stern and her five decks towered majestically above the dockyard area.

The *Noronic* was a happy ship. It was not only her last pleasure cruise of the season, but the voyage also marked the 36th year of the ship's service on the lakes. Carrying 524 passengers and 171 crewmen, *Noronic* had begun her final voyage in Detroit, crossed Lake Erie to Cleveland, spanned Lake Ontario and arrived at Toronto the evening of September 16, 1949.

From there, she would continue on to Kingston, Ontario, then thread her way through the picturesque Thousand Islands. But this night she would spend in Toronto to permit her passengers to go ashore.

By 1:30 A.M., most passengers had returned to the 6,700-ton cruiser. A few strolled the decks, some played cards in the ship's posh lounge. Others were asleep below or attending one of several festive parties in progress.

There was no hint of danger.

But within 15 minutes, a fire, believed to have started in a linen closet, would sweep the *Noronic*'s decks from bow to stern, reduce the ship to a gutted and blackened hulk and kill 120 passengers in one of the worst maritime disasters ever recorded in North America.

A pier watchman turned in the first alarm after seeing "a glimmer of flame near the stern." In six minutes, the first of 18 fire engines arrived, but by then almost the entire ship was ablaze.

Most of the passengers were asleep, but hundreds were able to escape in a frantic, screaming, pushing mob by jumping to the pier, into the water or clambering over the rails to smaller boats alongside.

But many others would find only death as they sought to escape the heat, smoke and flames.

Donald Church of Silver Lake, Ohio, was in the bar having a late drink.

"Somebody noticed flames coming out of a little laundry cupboard not far away," he said. "I called for someone to come from the purser's desk and a crewman came up with an extinguisher. Another crewman and I dragged a big fire hose about 20 feet to the

fire. It was turned on but only a few drops of water trickled out."

Survivors told graphic stories of how screaming, pushing men and women fought to get off the ship.

Sylvia Carpenter of Detroit saw smoke and flame billowing along the passageways. She said she screamed and headed for an outside rail.

"Someone had thrown a rope ladder over the dockside but it was all tangled," she said. "A rope was then tossed over the rail and I put a hitch knot on it to hold it to a stanchion. As I did so, three men pushed in front of me and shoved some screaming women out of the way. The three men went down the rope."

Another survivor, Alberta Agla, also of Detroit, described a "mob of men and women surging back and forth on deck. Men were pushing women around and many were knocked to the floor. The screaming filled the air. There was so much panic that I don't know how these people found a way to safety. I slid down a rope."

The master of the Noronic, Captain William Taylor, 66-year-old veteran of the Great Lakes, first learned of the fire when he went to his cabin after coming aboard the ship. A crew member ran by, shouting "Fire," and Captain Taylor, who had commanded the Noronic for the past eight years, ordered the ship's siren to be blown.

He then ran from stateroom to stateroom, pounding on doors with a fire hoze to try and awaken sleeping passengers.

Captain Taylor, who would first be proclaimed a hero, then later be blamed for taking inadequate fire precautions, stayed at his post for nearly half an hour before flames forced him to abandon ship. He leaped over the side and was fished out of the water by rescuers.

From the dock, firemen poured tons of water into the ship, but the fire was so hot that the water turned to steam as it hit the blazing decks.

Ben Kosman of Cleveland, one of the passengers who fled to safety, told of seeing ship attendants trying to stem the roaring flames with hand extinguishers.

"They might have been trying to put out hell with their fountain pens," he said.

Lucille Roberts of Detroit said she saw one man on an upper deck surrounded by flames. "As I watched, the flames licked around him and you could hear him scream

for the last time. Then he disappeared."

Whole families, vacationing on the Noronic's last cruise of the season, were wiped out. Most of the victims were from the Detroit and Cleveland areas. Firemen who finally got aboard the heat-twisted hulk five hours after the fire began told of finding charred groups with their arms about each other.

Edwin Feeney, a reporter for the Toronto Star, walked about the decks of the burned-out steamer and described a grisly scene:

"It was a horrible picture of charred remains amid foot-deep embers and melted glass. I saw the blackened bits that were once people. There was a young woman clutching her baby. . . .

"Many had their lives snuffed out without waking. One young woman, wrapped in a blanket, had her face burned but her body was not touched. Upper bunks fell crashing down on victims below. Firemen searching the ruins found human remains between scorched mattresses.

"There wasn't a wooden partition standing. There was no wooden furniture or upholstery unburned. No stairways remained save one at the bow of the ship. Every pane of glass had been melted by the intense heat."

Art Smith, a Toronto Fire Department official, said his men found victims in every position. "We found dozens of couples who went to death in a last embrace."

Smith said that steel stanchions were bent in every shape, and the decks, crumpled and buckled from the heat, made progress hazardous for the firemen seeking the dead.

"Never in my fire fighting days have I seen anything so ghastly, so tragic as this," Smith said.

The ship, with her name almost at pier level, went down at the stern, then settled by the bow. Her bridge and other parts of the wooden superstructure of her two upper decks were gone. The slip was filled with bobbing life belts. Steel lifeboats on the starboard side of the upper deck were crumpled.

Blackened wreckage, heaped on the main deck, looked like a burning coke pile, with rows of candle-like flame still flickering as firemen began bringing out the bodies, wrapped in tarpaulins.

The dead were taken to a temporary morgue set up in the horticultural building

**F**ire, believed to have started in a linen closet, is shown sweeping the bow and superstructure of the Canadian cruiser *Noronic*. The ship, in her 36th year of service on the Great Lakes, also was on her last pleasure cruise of the season.

of the Canadian National Exhibition four miles away. Bodies were piled up under the glass-domed roof of the building, where prize flowers had been on exhibit just a week before.

A special government court of inquiry was set up to investigate the fire which destroyed the $5 million ship and took so many lives.

K. R. Marshall, president of the Canadian Steamship Lines which owned the *Noronic,* said the ship was well equipped with modern fire fighting devices.

Marshall said the fire may have been started by a burning cigarette or cigar that had been left in an unattended room and added: "Certainly, none of the officers or crew knew of the fire until it became uncontrollable."

Some passengers, in testimony at the special inquiry, blamed the ship's officers for lack of leadership in the crisis. Crew members, however, blamed passengers for yielding to hysteria in trying to flee the ship.

Captain Taylor admitted, however, that neither he nor the steamship company had ever given written instructions to the crew on what to do in case of fire while the ship was docked.

When the investigation ended, a 30,000-word government report condemned the ship owners for failure to take proper precautions against fire, and censured Captain Taylor for failure to take an overall command role instead of "fighting the fire as an ordinary seaman."

The report also said the 15-man skeleton crew on board at the time was below the safety minimum.

The master's license of Captain Taylor was ordered suspended for a year, but the Ontario Attorney General's office said that evidence showed there was no foundation for any charges of criminal negligence against either Captain Taylor or the ship's owners.

In subsequent years, however, damage claims totaling nearly $3 million were awarded by the courts to survivors or families of victims.

**T**he charred remains of one of the below deck lounges (*top left*) gave mute testimony to the intensity of the fire. *Above left:* One of *Noronic*'s victims is removed by firemen from the still-smoking vessel.

**T**he body of a man, one of the *Noronic*'s passengers, is pulled from the waters of Toronto Bay. He apparently drowned while trying to escape from the searing flames which swept the ship. The body was recovered by a diver.

# UNSCHEDULED STOP AT RICHMOND HILL

This was the scene in Richmond Hill, Queens, when one Long Island Rail Road passenger train rammed into the rear of another train. The Thanksgiving Eve accident claimed 79 lives.

Wednesday evening, November 22, 1950. Thanksgiving eve. But there were those who wondered whether there was much to be thankful about.

The United States was involved in another war, this time in Korea, and American troops were pushing up close to the Manchurian border. And earlier in the month, there was an attempt to assassinate President Truman.

All over America on this Thanksgiving eve, people were flocking home with sober thoughts of world problems and men battling in bitter cold mountains somewhere in Asia.

A last-minute rush of air travel broke all previous records for this time of the year. In Pennsylvania Station, thousands waited to board trains bound for Long Island.

Train No. 780, headed for Hempstead, Long Island, left the Manhattan station at 6:09 P.M. On board were 1,000 passengers. A second train, No. 174, en route to Babylon, Long Island, with 1,200 passengers, left the lower concourse a few minutes later, at 6:13 P.M. Both trains were to stop at Jamaica, Long Island, as their first stop.

At the controls of the first train was Motorman William W. Murphy. Train No. 780 had stopped momentarily in the Richmond Hill section of Queens, on a section of track laid on an embankment about 15 feet above ground level. Then Murphy got the "go ahead" signal and was beginning to roll ahead at about 15 miles per hour, when suddenly the train faltered and stopped as the brakes "grabbed."

And in another few seconds, the Long Island Rail Road would experience the darkest day of its ill-starred career.

The Babylon express, which had been just minutes behind, hurtled headlong into the rear of Murphy's stopped train. In that grinding and shearing of steel, 79 commuters would die and more than 100 others

would be injured.

The rear of Murphy's train and the first car of the Babylon express were telescoped by the force of the impact.

Mr. and Mrs. William Staker were just sitting down to dinner when the collision occurred in front of their home.

"It sounded like an atomic bomb," Mrs. Staker said. "I thought at first the furnace had blown up. Then I ran outside, saw what happened and ran back to call the police and the hospitals."

William H. Good, 32-year-old member of the national advertising staff of *The New York Times,* was a passenger on the second train, headed for his home in Merrick, Long Island.

"I was in the eighth car when all of a sudden the brakes were jammed on," he related. "I was standing at the time and was thrown down the aisle. Some glass was broken in my car but I don't think anyone was hurt. The first car was smashed to pieces. It plowed under the rear one of the other."

Good said he heard no sounds coming from inside the smashed cars.

"I saw bloody hands hanging out of windows," he said. "They must have been dead, all of them. At first glance, I saw 10 bodies."

Not all of them.

David George and Robert Patterson, two executives of the railroad, were aboard the last car of No. 780. The impact knocked both of them out of their seats and onto the floor. Patterson was cut about the head.

"Our train made an emergency stop at 6:26 P.M.," George said. "Moments later there was a rending crash. We both lost consciousness and when we came to our senses in the darkness, we heard the screams and cries for help from trapped passengers."

Others weren't as fortunate as George

**T**wo hands of a mangled victim stick out grotesquely from between telescoped railroad cars as rescue workers attempt to free injured survivors. The two trains were packed with homeward-bound Long Island commuters.

and Patterson. In the twisted, shattered wreckage of the two cars, dozens lay dead, some so badly mangled that identification would be difficult. Some bodies were decapitated. Human limbs were scattered about.

For the Long Island Rail Road, the latest accident appeared to be a recurring nightmare. Only nine months before, on February 17, 32 persons were killed and more than 100 injured when two LIRR trains collided head-on near Rockville Centre, Long Island.

And the previous December 22, two empty passenger trains collided in Sunnyside, Queens, killing two crewmen and injuring six others. Ironically, the conductor and a crewman of the Babylon express, both of whom survived, also were involved in that earlier collision.

Recriminations over the operation of the Long Island Rail Road would fly fast and furious later. But for now, there was time only to tend the injured, rescue the trapped and remove the dead.

The police and fire departments rushed dozens of rescue units to the scene, and huge floodlights were set up to illuminate the disaster area. The cries of the injured mingled with the impatient shouts of the rescue workers as a subdued crowd of more than 5,000 people stood by, shocked by the enormity of the tragedy.

Priests administered last rites to the dying as white-coated doctors and ambulance attendants hurried from victim to victim dispensing morphine injections to those in pain and soothing the shocked and frightened with words of comfort.

As the night wore on and the cold became more penetrating, doctors and nurses draped blankets over their shoulders as they continued to treat the injured. Nearby homes were turned into emergency care centers.

Adding to the crowd were the relatives and friends of victims. Many wept openly as they waited for identification of the dead.

Rescue workers and equipment were moved into the area from all five city boroughs as well as neighboring Long Island communities. They worked far into the early morning hours trying to free victims entrapped in the twisted steel.

Two young hospital interns, Drs. Paul Soffer and Arnold Sanders, were credited with saving the lives of many of the injured. They crawled into the telescoped cars and for the next five hours they treated trapped passengers. When the two physicians finally crawled out of the wreckage they collapsed from exhaustion.

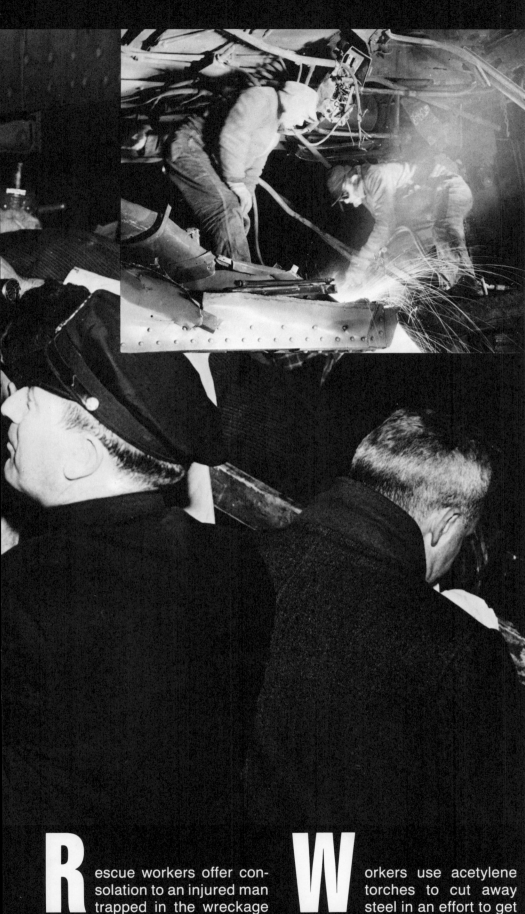

By dawn, all the dead had been removed and the injured dispersed to hospitals throughout the Queens area. Even the debris had been cleaned away. The only evidence of the carnage of the night before was a torn bit of bandage near the railroad right of way, a discarded baby blanket hanging on a wire fence and a backyard garden that had been trampled under the feet of rescue workers and onlookers.

Even as the last of the dead were being removed from the wreckage, Acting Mayor of New York Joseph Sharkey declared:

"Something must be done to stop this carnage. If public ownership is the answer, that's it."

He called for a unified investigation by state and city agencies "to get to the bottom of this and learn why these things must happen on this particular line. It's about time that we should find out the cause of these wrecks on the Long Island Rail Road."

"Something must be done quickly in the interests of public safety. I'm not interested in the financial operations of the road but in the safety of the people," Sharkey added.

Queens District Attorney Charles Sullivan demanded that the city and state take over what he termed the "Death Valley Railroad," then operated as a debt-ridden and bankrupt subsidiary of the Pennsylvania Railroad.

Several days after the accident, LIRR officials would blame the disaster on "human error." They said that the motorman of the Babylon express, 55-year-old Benjamin Pokorney, may have missed the warning signals and was at a speed "beyond the margin of safety." It was estimated that the Babylon express was running at about 60 miles an hour before Pokorney applied the emergency brakes.

But Pokorney was unable to defend himself during the investigation. He had died at the controls of his train.

Both New York Governor Thomas Dewey and Mayor Vincent Impellitteri joined as one voice in demanding that the trustees of the Long Island Rail Road resign. Dewey added that the latest wreck was a "heart-rendering demonstration that drastic action is necessary for the safety of the people of our state who used that railroad." Drastic action was taken.

The Long Island Rail Road eventually came under public ownership and its commuter facilities are currently operated by the Metropolitan Transportation Authority. But public confidence in the line was never fully restored.

**R**escue workers offer consolation to an injured man trapped in the wreckage of the two railroad cars. The two cars are being jacked apart in an effort to free him and others trapped in the mass of twisted steel.

**W**orkers use acetylene torches to cut away steel in an effort to get to those still trapped in the cars. Many victims were mangled beyond recognition in the grinding crash.

**P**olicemen stand over the bodies of several dead, removed from the wrecked trains and laid in the street to await removal to a morgue. The accident was the worst in the ill-starred history of the Long Island Rail Road.

**T**he emergency ward of Queens General Hospital is a scene of frantic activity as doctors and nurses work over scores of injured taken there after the train collision.

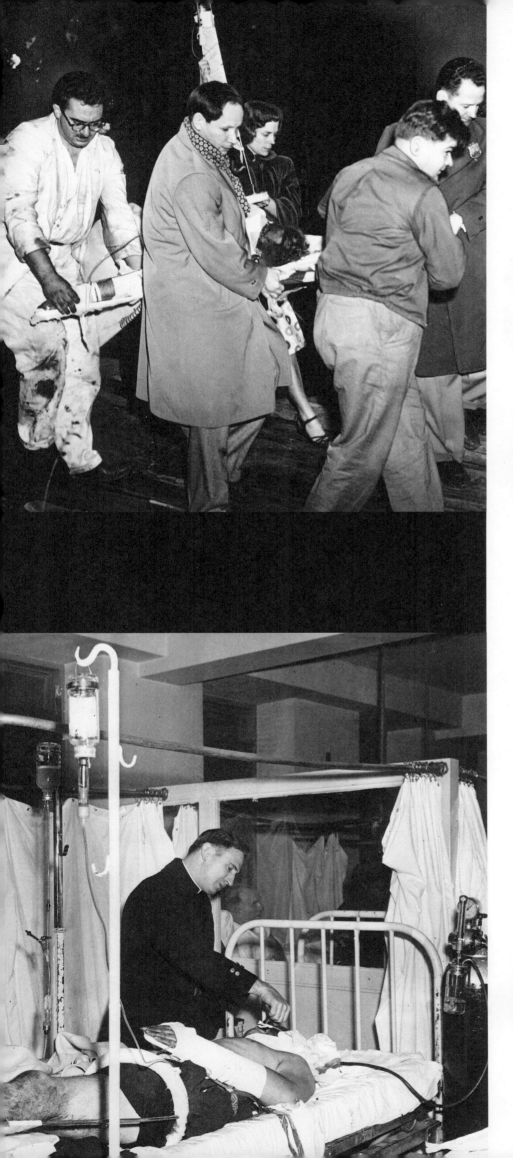

**A** doctor, his clothes blackened from efforts in aiding victims in the train collision, helps remove an injured man to a waiting ambulance.

**A** priest administers last rites to one of the more severely injured.

# LEGEND OF THE HUACOS

In one minute on May 11, 1953, a massive tornado destroyed two square miles of Waco, Texas, reducing large buildings to rubble. Several people died when they were crushed inside their automobiles by falling buildings.

The city of Waco is the last place in Texas a tornado should strike, according to the Huaco Indians, for whom the city is named. They said it would never happen.

But that was generations ago, when settlers were choosing a site for a new village amid the rolling and wooded hills of central Texas.

On Monday, May 11, 1953, the legend of the Huacos came to a sickening end in the fury of a deadly tornado that smashed into downtown Waco with the force of a giant scythe and left behind a swath of death and destruction. In one terrible minute, the massive twister turned the city of 90,000 persons into a jumble of wreckage and a death trap for 114. Hundreds more were injured, and nearly $60 million in damage was counted.

The tornado roared in just before the 5 P.M. rush hour, touching down twice, once in a residential area and then in the heart of the city. It was the downtown area that caught the full brunt of the deadly winds.

Within seconds, two square miles of Waco were destroyed or heavily damaged; it looked like a city gutted by war.

The dead were killed by tumbling buildings, flying brick and other debris. Some died sitting in their automobiles, buried under tons of falling stone. And some were buried alive, but lived to tell about it.

John William Coates had been talking on the telephone to his pretty, red-haired wife. Coates, who worked in a paint store operated by his father-in-law, had called home to warn his wife of the storm. He described the darkness, the heavy rain and light hailstones in the downtown area.

Then his words turned into a scream. "Honey, the building's falling in!" And the telephone line went dead. That was the last word Mrs. Coates had until her husband's lifeless body was recovered from the wreckage of the paint store the following night. The bodies of her father and mother, who also were in the store, were found a little later.

The five-story R. T. Dennis Building (*top*), tallest structure in Waco, was nearly flattened to ground level by the vicious twister. A number of workers inside the building perished. *Above:* This aerial view of Waco's business district shows the extent of the devastation.

**R**escue workers keep up the spirits of a 17-year-old boy, trapped beneath rubble that was once a pool hall in downtown Waco. The youngster later was rescued, but 17 others in the hall died.

Two hours earlier, a twister had struck the city of San Angelo, 200 miles to the west, but that city was lucky by comparison. Ten persons died there.

But perhaps to give mockery to the old Indian legend, the storm vented its full fury on Waco, where it left a twisted mass of crumpled steel and broken concrete.

The tornado struck in a blinding rainstorm. The approach was so silent that some victims got their first warning from a horrible suction that lifted them off their feet and slammed them into crumbling buildings.

The dead and injured were pulled from flattened buildings, from crushed cars, from under fallen power poles and twisted signs, and even from swimming pools.

Motorcycle patrolman Al Blackwell said he saw the funnel forming about 10 miles southwest of Waco. "It was a narrow funnel, but it got bigger and bigger and I saw it dip down in town," he said.

The twister struck hardest around Waco's town square, destroying or damaging every building within about a 20-block area.

A giant steel and wood bridge spanning the Brazos River offered mute testimony to the force of the destructive winds. The steel sides of the span were sliced open as if by a giant can opener. The wood sections were turned into kindling.

Eighteen-year-old Lonnie Murphree was in the Torrance Recreation Hall, a public pool parlor, with 28 others, mostly teenagers like himself, when the tornado struck.

"We were all playing pool," Murphree said, "when the lights went out. Nobody paid much attention. We just thought it was the storm. It was raining and hail was beating down on the windows.

"The dust began to come down from the ceiling and that's when I figured something was wrong. I dived under a pool table and almost everyone else did, too. After a while, I pushed away brick and stuff and crawled out. I looked around and saw this awful, awful mess."

Of the 29 young people in the pool hall, 12 were able to get out or were rescued. The other 17 lay crushed under tons of debris.

Some had to wait hours before rescue. Donald Hansard, a 17-year-old Levega, Texas, high school football star, lay trapped in the pool hall wreckage for nearly seven hours.

Hansard dived under a pool table as the building collapsed. As he lay under a tiny air hole, only the side of his face could be seen as rescuers dug frantically to free him.

His father, Aubrey Hansard, sat at the air hole and held a flashlight on his son's face. "Don't go to sleep—I won't let you go to sleep," he kept repeating to his son.

Phil Hardberger, a Baylor University student who had been in the pool hall but had left before the tornado struck, broke through the wreckage to help free Hansard.

"I saw eight dead," he said after the rescue. "And I saw the attendant with his hand outstretched as if to collect for a game. Beside him was a guy with 10 cents still in his hand. Two others were in a kneeling position as if they were trying to protect themselves from the falling building." All were dead.

Martial law was declared and guards armed with carbines and pistols patrolled the devastated area to protect against looting, as hundreds of rescue workers raced against time in their search for possible survivors buried under the rubble.

A number of victims were found in what was left of the five-story R.T. Dennis Building, which was razed almost to ground level.

When a crane lifted a section of the wall the next day, rescuers made a gruesome discovery: The bodies of two women who worked in the building were found firmly imbedded in the wall.

A Baylor professor, Keith W. James, and his wife were found in the wreckage of their car nearby, crushed under debris from the Dennis Building. The bodies of three high school girls also were found in the remains of their car where they apparently sat to wait out the storm.

Meanwhile, the injured poured into hospitals so fast that doctors and nurses at one point had time only to slap a piece of adhesive tape on foreheads, scribble a name on it and give the injured person a shot to ease the pain.

Mercedes Carbajal was ill with polio and flat on her back in the trailer house belonging to her brother-in-law when the twister struck. Two of her five children were in the Carbajal's frame home next door, the other three were staying with relatives.

Mrs. Carbajal said that when the tornado hit, "I knew something happened to my house, maybe to my children. I jumped up and ran to the door." Her home was demolished, but her children escaped unhurt. Before the storm, she could move her legs, but could not stand. "Terror enabled me to walk again," she said.

Today, Waco is a modern city with no scars left from the fateful Monday. The devil wind is now mostly a memory—along with the legend of the Huacos.

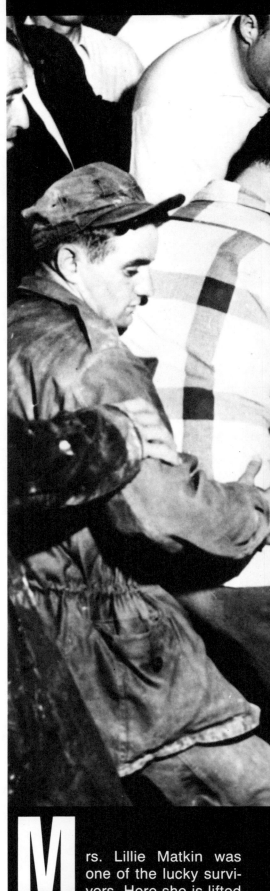

**M**rs. Lillie Matkin was one of the lucky survivors. Here she is lifted by rescuers from the wreckage of the R. T. Dennis Building, where she had been pinned overnight.

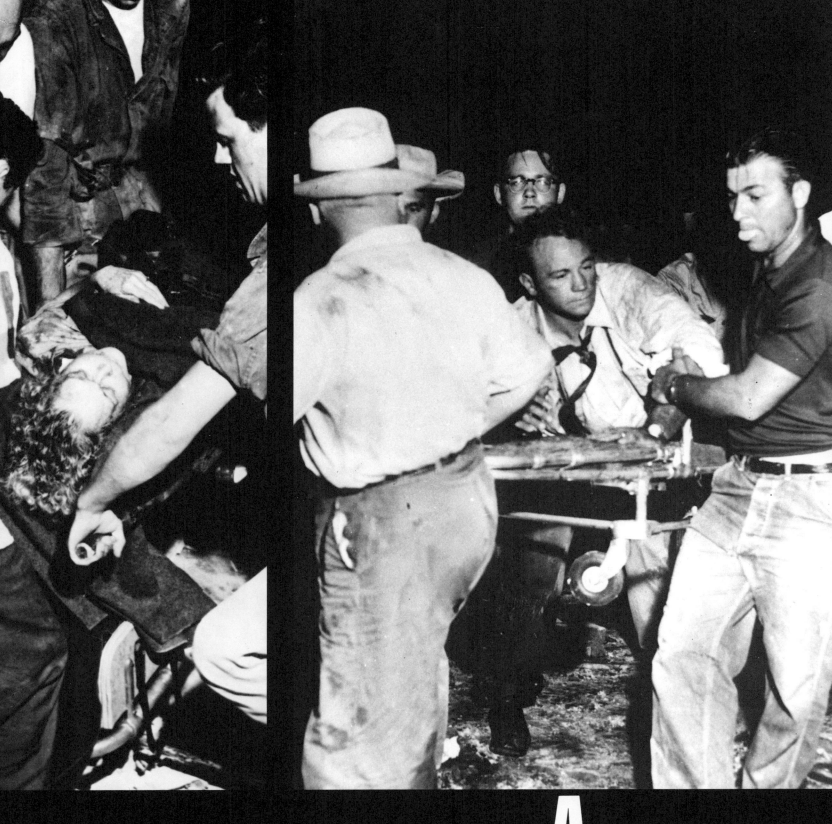

An unidentified man, his face registering the ordeal he has undergone, is lifted out of tornado debris by rescue workers. He had been trapped in the wreckage for 12 hours.

# COLLISION
# AT SEA

**T**his dramatic low-level air view shows the *Andrea Doria* heeling far over to starboard just before sinking to the bottom of the Atlantic off Nantucket Island.

Andrea Doria-
Stockholm
Collision

The fog off Nantucket was thicker than usual the night of July 25, 1956. It rose like steam from contact between the warm night air and the cooler sea. A very faint breeze was blowing across the ocean.

The sleek Italian liner *Andrea Doria,* under command of Captain Piero Calamai, rode gracefully over a gentle swell as she pushed steadily through the murk, 200 miles from New York, inbound.

Shortly after 11 P.M., 15-year-old Martin Sejda, a passenger, left the ship's brilliantly lighted main ballroom and went out on deck for a stroll.

He found himself in a sightless world; thick veils of fog mantled the ship, blotting out sea and sky. Sejda could barely see the outlines of the rail just across the deck. As he felt his way toward it, the ship's whistle roared, sending out a hoarse-voiced fog warning.

Five miles away, on an outbound course, was the trim, white-painted Swedish motorship *Stockholm.* Both ships had modern radar, capable of "seeing" each other at that short range.

In the ballroom of the *Doria,* the orchestra began playing "Arrivederci Roma," a song that had become a favorite on the voyage. People rose to dance, among them Ruth Roman, pretty, dark-haired motion picture actress.

Nearby, in the cardroom, Stanley Sagner of Baltimore, Maryland, was chortling over the score of a gin rummy game with his friend, Irving Perellis. Across the room, three Standard Oil executives—Dr. Stewart Coleman of Long Island, New York, Marion W. Boyer of Greenwich, Connecticut, and H. G. Burks of Elizabeth, New Jersey—and their wives were holding a post-mortem on a hand of bridge that had just been played.

Below decks, the movie "Fox Fire" was just about over. But John Dozzo, 77, and his wife, Carmela, had skipped the picture. For the elderly couple this was their honeymoon trip after two weeks of marriage. They were laughing now as they packed their wedding gifts.

Everyone aboard agreed that it had been a good voyage. The ship had sailed from Genoa July 17, with stops at Naples, Cannes and Gibraltar, before heading westward into the open Atlantic.

At Gibraltar, *New York Times* correspondent Camille Cianfarra, 49, had come aboard with his family. He had tried to book passage on the *Cristoforo Columbo,* sister ship of the *Andrea Doria.* But unable to get accommodations, he took passage on the *Doria.* With his wife, Jane, his daughter, Joan, and his stepdaughter, Linda Morgan, he obtained cabins on an upper deck.

Now the voyage was nearly ended. This was the night before landing and the usual last-night atmosphere—a mixture of the bitter and sweet, relief and regret—settled over the *Andrea Doria.* Many passengers, in fact, had gone to bed earlier than usual.

Aboard the motorship *Stockholm,* seaman Arne Smedberg had just sunk into bed with a luxurious sigh. His bunk was well forward, near the bow.

The Swedish ship, commanded by Captain Gunnar Nordenson, had not altered course. Neither had the *Andrea Doria.*

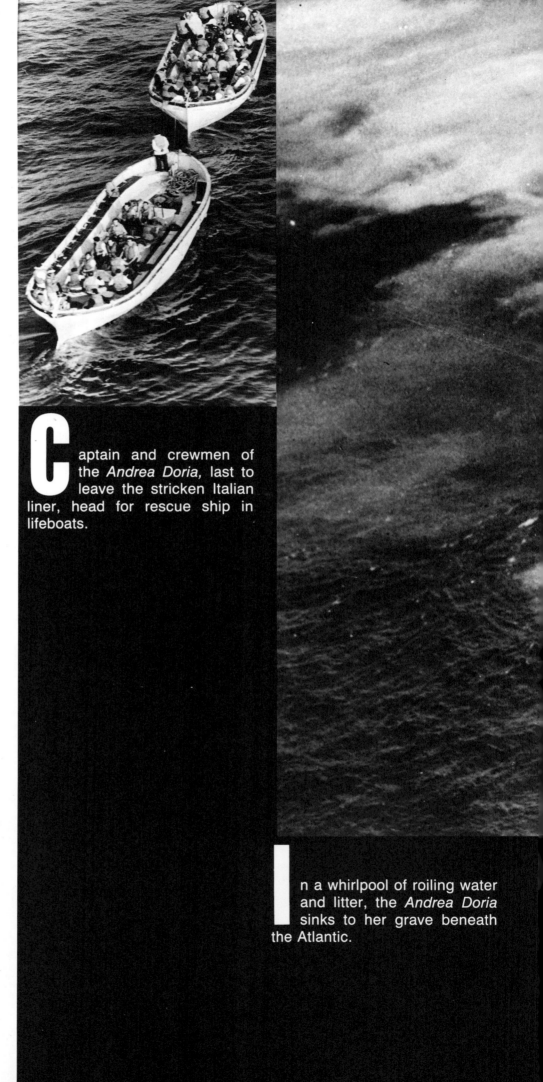

Captain and crewmen of the *Andrea Doria,* last to leave the stricken Italian liner, head for rescue ship in lifeboats.

In a whirlpool of roiling water and litter, the *Andrea Doria* sinks to her grave beneath the Atlantic.

On the deck of the Italian vessel, young Martin Sejda was getting sleepy and he decided to join his parents in the ballroom. As he started to turn away from the rail, he saw something that froze him: the lights of the liner *Stockholm*.

"I saw her lights about three seconds before the crash. The ship was coming in at an angle like it was trying to keep from hitting us," he said.

In a cabin below decks, Mary Marsich of Cleveland, Ohio, was asleep. Her friend, Frances Aljinovic, happened to glance through the porthole. What she saw made her gasp.

"I saw the boat alongside us. It was all lighted up. It was very close and getting closer. I said, 'Mary, it's going to hit,' and it did."

At 11:20 P.M. the *Stockholm*'s graceful bow, heavily reinforced against possible ice in northern waters, tore a jagged hole in *Andrea Doria*'s starboard side just behind the bridge. The hole was 40 feet across at its widest point.

The *Stockholm*'s bow was torn, bent and folded back like a mashed tin can. But her wound was not mortal.

The *Andrea Doria*'s was. The first large swell sent tons of water pouring in and, almost immediately, she began to list.

In that awful instant, death came swiftly to some on both ships.

In No. 46 cabin on the *Doria*'s upper deck, Walter Carlin, well known in Brooklyn Democratic circles, had just stepped into the corridor on his way to meet some friends. His wife had gone to bed. The crash knocked Carlin off his feet and when he staggered back into his cabin, he saw a gaping hole in the ship's side. His wife vanished.

In Cabins 52-54, Camille Cianfarra and his daughter, Joan, 8, apparently were crushed to death instantly. Mrs. Cianfarra was jammed between the bulkhead and a spring of her bed. Linda, her other daughter, was missing.

In a nearby cabin, Dr. Thure Peterson, a 57-year-old chiropractor, was hurled out of bed clear across the room and slammed into unconsciousness against a wall. When he came to, he heard screaming and cries for help. He found his wife pinned against the bulkhead, her back and both legs broken. He gave her morphine, and with the help of another passenger tried to free her, but failed.

Peterson heard Mrs. Cianfarra's cries for help. The doctor and the other man cut her free, then returned to the chiropractor's cabin to make another attempt at freeing

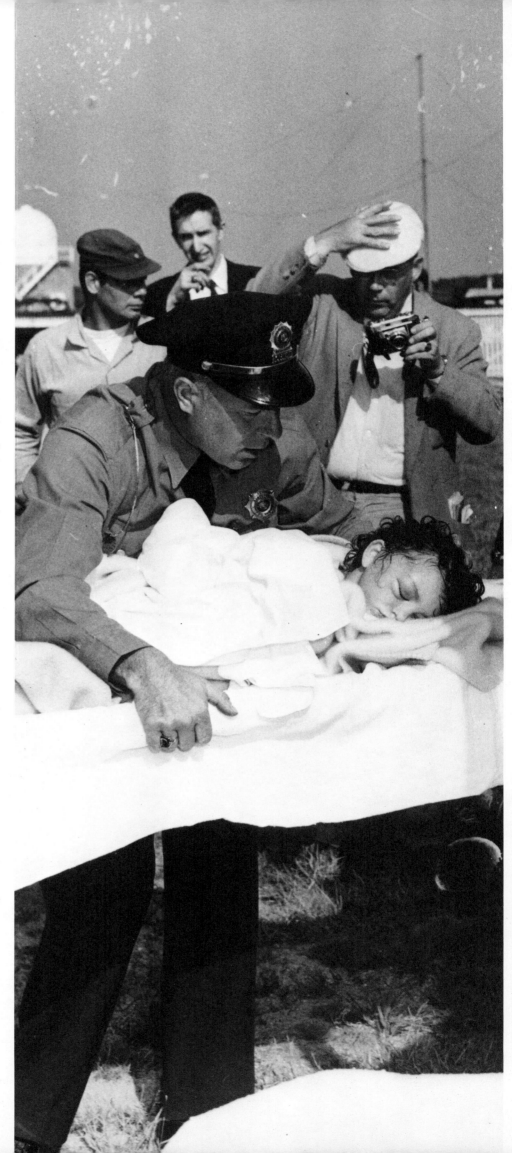

**A**n unidentified 7-year-old girl, injured in the collision, is placed aboard an ambulance in Boston after being taken from the *Stockholm* by helicopter.

Mrs. Peterson. But she was already dead.

Mayor Richardson Dilworth of Philadelphia and his wife had gone to bed several hours before the collision. Both were thrown to the floor of their cabin by the impact, then they fled to an upper deck.

Actress Ruth Roman fought her way through crowds to the room where her 3½-year-old son, Dickie, lay sleeping. He had not even awakened. The actress nudged him up and told him: "We're going on a picnic."

On board the *Stockholm,* five sailors asleep in the forward part of the ship were killed instantly. Seaman Smedberg, however, survived.

"The first thing I knew, everything seemed to cave in," he said. "Things were falling. It was like lightning striking."

Maritime listening posts heard a chilling exchange of messages starting at 11:22 P.M.

11:22 (From the *Stockholm*): "We have collided with another ship. Please. Ship in collision."

11:25 (From the Coast Guard): "*Andrea Doria* and *Stockholm* collided. Latitude 40-30 North, Longitude 69-53 West."

11:30 (*Stockholm* to *Andrea Doria*): "If you can lower lifeboats, we can pick you up."

11:35 (*Andrea Doria* to *Stockholm*): "We are bending (listing) . . . impossible . . . put lifeboats at sea . . . send immediate assistance . . . lifeboats."

Then a few moments later, the dreaded "SOS"—extreme emergency signal—was sounded by the *Andrea Doria.* Instantly, scores of craft, big and small, pointed their bows toward the area in which the Coast Guard said the accident had occurred.

At stake: the rescue of 1,134 passengers and 575 crewmen on the *Doria,* 750 passengers and crew of the *Stockholm.*

About 50 miles away, the great French liner *Ile de France,* under command of Captain Raoul de Beaudean, altered course as soon as the SOS was heard and sped at 22 knots through fog and arrived at the collision scene in under two hours.

"I prayed for a miracle," said Captain de Beaudean. It was granted. On the way to the scene, the fog lifted. The French ship came in with her lifeboats already swung out from davits, ready for lowering. Passengers on the *Andrea Doria,* who could see the arrival of *Ile de France* now that the fog had thinned, burst into cheers and tears.

Except for some struggling between passengers trying to get down to their cabins

**C**harles Dazzo greets his mother with a tearful embrace. Mrs. Dazzo and her husband arrived in New York aboard the *Ile de France* with 700 other survivors of the Italian liner.

after the crash and those struggling up from below, there was no panic. But the ship soon canted over at such a sharp angle that it became impossible to walk upright either through corridors or on deck.

Once out on deck, passengers either went down webbed rope ladders to waiting lifeboats, or simply slid down the oily side of the ship. Passengers and crew together formed a human chain to help women, children and older people down the steep, slippery side.

Two-year-old Maria Dooner slipped and fell into the sea. Instantly, her mother, a strong swimmer, dove over the side after her. Mrs. Dooner grabbed the little girl and both were picked up by a lifeboat.

Tulio de Sandro threw his 4-year-old daughter into the arms of a stranger in one of the lifeboats. It pulled away without him.

Across a quarter-mile of water, the lights of *Ile de France* blazed brightly on the scene. More ships kept arriving, and more lifeboats plied back and forth until almost all of the *Doria*'s nearly 1,700 survivors had been taken off.

Finally, at 4:58 A.M., the *Ile de France* radioed: "All passengers rescued. Proceeding to New York full speed."

The master of the *Andrea Doria,* Captain Calamai, and a group of his senior officers stayed aboard the dying ship in an attempt to save her. For a time, it seemed that her pumps might stave off the inrushing water. But it was not to be.

Toward dawn, Captain Calamai left the ship. By 8:30 A.M., water was lapping over her starboard rail and one giant propeller jutted out of the water. A few minutes after 10, the pride of the Italian merchant fleet began to sink along her entire length. A burst of foam and bubbles surged up as she went under.

The *Andrea Doria,* called a "floating art gallery" because of her beautiful art decor, was gone, buried under 200 feet of water. Under Navy escort, the *Stockholm* limped back to New York.

But mercy and tragedy would continue to walk together.

Young Martin Sejda and the card-playing passengers of the opening scenes of the drama survived the collision.

Tulio de Sandro, who threw his small daughter into a lifeboat, found her in a Boston hospital, gravely injured. She died later—one of 50 to perish in the collision between the two ships.

But 14-year-old Linda Morgan, stepdaughter of Camille Cianfarra, arrived on a rescue ship. "I was thrown out of my cabin—or something," she said. "I don't remember what else happened."

Later, millions of dollars in claims would be filed against both ship lines. But the burning question—which ship was responsible for the collision—was never answered. Attempts to fix blame in court were abandoned by both lines.

The *Stockholm* returned to sea after being fitted with a new bow, at a cost of $1 million. The *Andrea Doria* remains on the bottom of the Atlantic Ocean. Divers have probed her watery compartments, but critical details on the collision remain unresolved.

**H**ere is an artist's conception of the collision between the *Doria* and the Swedish liner *Stockholm.* The *Stockholm,* at left, with her bow stove in, has backed off and let down her lifeboats. The *Andrea Doria* is already alist with a gaping hole in her starboard side.

**T**he liner *Stockholm,* her bow a mass of crumpled steel, is shown in a Brooklyn, New York, shipyard several days after her collision at sea with the *Andrea Doria.*

# A CHRISTMAS REUNION

The bodies of victims lie on a sidewalk not far from where their jet airplane turned a quiet Brooklyn street into a holocaust.

0       10 Miles

NEW

JERSEY

NEWARK

Newark
Airport

BRONX

LaGuardia
Airport

Hudson

MANHATTAN

QUEENS

Upper
Bay

United Air Lines
Crash

Idlewild
Airport

TWA Flight Path

STATEN

LINDEN
INTERSECTION

ISLAND

Miller Field

New Dorp

TWA Crash

BROOKLYN

Floyd Bennett
Field

Lower
Bay

Atlantic

Ocean

United Air Lines Flight Path

PRESTON
INTERSECTION

Eleven-year-old Steven Baltz of Wilmette, Illinois, was a happy youngster the morning of December 16, 1960, when he boarded United Air Lines Flight 826 in Chicago's O'Hare Airport.

The big DC-8 jet, carrying 77 passengers and a crew of seven, was headed for New York's Idlewild Airport (now known as Kennedy International Airport), where he would be met by his mother and sister.

Steven, out of school for the Christmas holidays, was to visit with his grandparents in Yonkers, New York, for a few days of shopping and sightseeing, then return to Wilmette with his mother and sister to spend Christmas at home.

He was to have flown to New York two days earlier, but a cold and sore throat had kept him in bed.

At about the same time as Steven was boarding, Trans World Airlines Flight 266, a propeller-driven Constellation, took off from Dayton, Ohio, bound for LaGuardia Airport in New York with 39 passengers and a crew of five.

Most of the passengers on both planes were holiday travelers, bearing gayly wrapped packages for relatives and friends.

Approaching New York City, the United jet was ordered by traffic controllers to fly a holding pattern 5,000 feet over Preston, New Jersey, until cleared to proceed to Idlewild. The TWA plane was directed to fly a holding pattern 6,000 feet over Linden, New Jersey, until cleared for LaGuardia.

Both aircraft were on instrument approaches because fog and sleet had reduced ground visibility to only 600 feet.

Airport radar operators had blips of both planes on their scopes. Suddenly, the blips came together, then disappeared from the screens as air controllers looked on helplessly. The worst had happened.

Both planes, apparently flying at the same altitude, collided in the air above the Narrows, a heavily traveled steamship lane between Brooklyn and Staten Island.

The United jet plunged out of the sky toward the populous Park Slope area of Brooklyn. It narrowly missed a parochial school where more than 1,000 children were in class, sheared off the steeply gabled roof of the Pillar of Fire Church, then scoured a block-wide area with fiery destruction.

Ironically, a large section of the jetliner came to rest in the wreckage of a Brooklyn funeral parlor, with more than a score of passengers entombed in the debris of the house of death.

The four-engine Constellation apparently exploded in the air. Parts of the plane fell on Miller Army Air Field, near New Dorp, Staten Island, 11 miles southwest from where the United jet was turning a quiet Brooklyn street into a holocaust.

It was, to date, the worst air disaster in the history of aviation.

Of 128 people aboard the planes, the sole survivor was one small boy—Steven Baltz. Six other persons died on the ground, including a street cleaner who was shoveling snow, and two Christmas tree merchants who were setting up their trees outside a store.

Young Steven was thrown from the tail section of the jetliner and hurled into a snowbank, his clothes aflame. Police and several others rushed to the youngster's aid. They rolled Steven in the snow to put out his blazing clothing.

A block away, in St. John's Episcopal Church, the Reverend Harry Stirling had just completed a Mass when an explosion shook the candlesticks.

"I went to the gate and there was a policeman running down the street," he said. "I hurried to Seventh Avenue and saw the burning plane. The boy was lying in the snow, terribly hurt but still alive. His face, part of his hair and his eyelashes were badly burned. He kept holding up his right arm and the hand was bleeding."

Steven was rushed to a nearby hospital, in critical condition from burns, broken bones and other injuries. While in the emergency room, he told doctors that he had held onto his seat as the jet hurtled toward the ground. "That's all I remember until I woke up here," he said.

But the joy of Steven's parents over his survival would be short lived. The youngster died of injuries 24 hours later.

Even as doctors worked desperately on the boy in an effort to save his life, firemen and police still did not know they were dealing with the crash of a jetliner. They thought at first that a prop plane had crashed and that

**F**iremen pour water into a burning apartment house set afire by the crash of a United jet. Parts of the aircraft lie in the street.

**T**he huge tail section of a United Air Lines DC-8 rests at a Brooklyn, New York, intersection. The airliner crashed after colliding with another plane.

**A** policeman stands guard (*top*) at the wrecked tail section and part of the fuselage of the TWA Constellation that crashed on Miller Army Air Field, Staten Island. *Above:* Blanketed bodies of victims mark the grim aftermath of tragedy.

no more than a dozen persons were aboard. Not until aviation accident investigators got to the scene did the extent of the disaster become apparent.

Brooklyn resident and eyewitness Salvatore Manza had been shoveling snow when he heard a whistling sound and looked up.

"I saw this plane coming from there toward there," he said, pointing from southwest to northeast. "All of a sudden, the right wing dipped. It hooked into the corner of an apartment house roof, and the rest of the plane slammed into the church and the apartment house across the street. All at once everything was on fire, and the fire from the plane in the street was as high as the houses."

In the third-floor quarters above the McCaddin Funeral Home, Mr. and Mrs. Henry McCaddin were having a mid-morning cup of coffee. Their year-old daughter, Donna, was playing under the kitchen table.

"We were having our coffee and I said to Henry, 'My goodness, that plane sounds awfully low,'" Mrs. McCaddin related. "And just then the whole house shook like it had been hit by a bomb, and the room was all flames.

"I started to grab the baby, and I saw Mr. Carter run in. He grabbed the baby and somehow we all got out."

The Mr. Carter who rescued the child was 29-year-old Robert Carter, who ran a beauty salon across the street from the funeral home.

"I saw the flames coming out of McCaddin's and I ran over," Carter said. "Afterward, I tried to get near the wreckage of the plane, but the fire was so bad it singed my eyebrows."

Priests from nearby St. Augustine's Parochial School ran to the scene, but found the intersection ablaze with burning jet fuel. Flaming rivulets raced down the slope of Sterling Place and enveloped parked automobiles, setting off a chain of popping explosions as gas tanks erupted.

The Reverend Raymond Morgan, assistant pastor of St. Augustine's, said, "The heat was terrific and the flames were shooting three stories high. We couldn't get near the plane, so we helped people out of threatened houses. We heard no screams from the wreckage."

On Staten Island, scores of people saw

the death throes of the TWA Constellation as it plunged to earth.

The flaming forward section of the aircraft, from which 29 bodies were taken, smashed into the northwest corner of the Miller Army Air Field, less than 150 feet away from the frame home of Mr. and Mrs. Edward Brody.

"I saw it coming right at us," Mrs. Brody said. "I ran upstairs to get my daughters. Then it stopped."

A 30-foot wing section and one engine swirled out of the overcast 50 feet from a row of frame officers' quarters at the field.

And the rear half of the fuselage spun to earth about 100 yards from the home of Mrs. John Barry. She picked up her 6-month-old daughter and plunged, in panic, through still, heavy snow.

About 1,000 pupils were in classes at Public School 41, two blocks away, when debris landed in the schoolyard.

Other wreckage was spread over a square mile. Twisted and burned shards of metal weighing as much as 50 pounds slammed onto a busy boulevard nearby and fell into yards and driveways. That no one was hurt on the ground and that no homes had been hit was a wonder.

But the grim panorama of death was everywhere. The body of a passenger hung from a tree along the boulevard; others were sprawled in the snow several hundred yards from the tail section.

The horror of the death plunge was graphically described by Clifford Beuth, an oil deliveryman.

"I saw the engine on the right side blow up. Then the second engine on the right side blew up, and as it did, it blew the tail section to pieces. I saw a couple of people falling out of the plane as it was falling. The plane was on fire from the time it blew up to the time it crashed."

It was only the second in-flight collision ever recorded between commercial airliners—but it had its share of coincidences. The previous aerial collision occurred in 1956 over Grand Canyon in Arizona. Then also, 128 people died. Then also, it involved aircraft owned by United and TWA.

But the awesome tragedy which occurred over New York City pointed up the growing peril of over-crowded airways above the nation's larger cities.

**R**esidents of a nearby tenement evacuate their apartments after the crash of an airliner in Brooklyn.

**139**

**S**heltered by an umbrella, 11-year-old Steven Baltz of Wilmette, Illinois, lies critically injured on a pile of snow not far from the wreckage of the airliner. He was the sole survivor of the two planes which collided over New York City, but died of his injuries 24 hours later.

**S**pectators register varying degrees of shock as victims of airliner crash are carried off Brooklyn street by police.

# IT'S HOW YOU PLAY THE GAME

**P**anicky soccer fans pushed themselves into a struggling mass in an attempt to avoid police tear gas. It turned into a death scramble for hundreds of men, women and children who had gone to National Stadium in Lima for the Argentina-Peru match.

**I**n an effort to keep the fans at bay, police, including one leading a guard dog, lobbed tear gas grenades toward the crowded stands. It didn't stop the unruly mob.

PERU

ECUADOR

BRAZIL

Lima ✠ Soccer Riot

BOLIVIA

0          500 Miles

Latin Americans have always played soccer with the same kind of fury they put into revolutions. In fact, police precautions are taken at major matches to keep excitable fans under control.

Perhaps the most spectacular safeguard is at Rio de Janeiro's Maracana Stadium, with a seating capacity of 100,000. A moat surrounds the playing field to keep angry fans away. Drawbridges permit entry of the players and officials on the field, and if trouble starts, the bridges are raised.

The playing field at National Stadium in Lima, Peru, is surrounded by a nine-foot chain link fence topped by barbed wire and backed up by a thick brick retaining wall—all to keep fans from charging down from the stands in large, angry numbers and falling upon a hapless referee, a visiting player or one of their own.

In Lima, on Sunday, May 24, 1964—a chilly and misty day—about 45,000 taut and nervous fans were seated behind the chain link fence watching a most important game. Peru was playing Argentina and at stake was a chance to go to the Olympics in Tokyo.

There was no doubt whose side the fans were on. The slightest success by a Peruvian player was met with wild enthusiasm. And when the Argentineans scored the first goal of the game, the silence was deafening.

Then with only 10 minutes left to play, the Argentine-Peru soccer rivalry turned into the worst tragedy in the history of sports.

An Argentine halfback inadvertently booted the ball into his own net and the hometown crowd went wild with joy, thinking the score was now tied.

Then, suddenly, joy turned to dismay; the referee, Angel Eduardo Pazos, a Uruguayan, disallowed the goal, ruling the Argentine player had been fouled by a member of the Peru team.

The Peruvian players protested mildly and play continued. But in the stands, the jeers and boos and whistles mounted. Here and there, bottles and rocks—anything the fans could lay their hands on—began sailing out onto the field, and the wave of anger was now spreading through the crowd.

It would take only a small incident to unleash all hell's fury. That incident would be set off by a husky black partisan known as "Bomba"—"The Bomb."

With five minutes left in the game "Bomba," who earned his nickname because of his previous attacks on referees, scrambled over the protective fence at the south end of the field as the crowd yelled, "¡Ahí va Bomba!" "There goes The Bomb."

**A** tangle of bodies lies in a heap in one of the tunnels leading from National Stadium in Lima, Peru. They died in their panic to escape choking tear gas.

"Bomba" charged at the referee, screaming insults. But the police were able to grab him and hustle him off the field. Then another man ran onto the field and the police collared him, too. But suddenly the spectators were pouring onto the field in angry waves. There was no stopping them.

Referee Pazos quickly called the game, ruled Argentina the winner and fled for his life into a steel-doored dressing room. The players also escaped unharmed.

But still the crowd kept coming. And deprived of the object of its fury—the referee—it exploded into riot and destruction.

The protective fence surrounding the stadium field was knocked down and torn into pieces by bare hands. Wooden stands at one end of the field were set afire.

A band of 40 policemen inside the stadium began lobbing tear gas in an effort to break up the unruly crowd. Fury now turned to panic.

Fans raced into the stadium tunnels, piling one on another, screaming, crying for help. Many smothered, some fell and were trampled to death.

Part of the crowd fled through the south gates; at the north end of the field, however, the gates—customarily opened 15 minutes before the end of the match—remained locked.

The first wave of fleeing spectators crashed against the gates. The second wave crashed against the first. Then there was a third wave, a fourth, a fifth—the gates still held firmly.

The dead and the dying began to pile up against the north exits. Some were crushed; some trampled; some asphyxiated.

"They came at us like a wave in a bad sea," said 37-year-old fisherman Leonardo Cevallos, who had brought his whole family to the big game. Cevallos survived. But his wife and five children died in the panic.

Propelled by an animal fear, others began to climb the rising hill of bodies at the north gates, only to fall back and become part of the pile.

Finally, mercifully, the gates weakened and sprang open. Screaming, gasping for air, wild-eyed with terror, the survivors began to escape the awful trap. They climbed over the piles of bodies, stumbled into the fresh air and the street and kept on running.

Part of the huge crowd which remained in the stadium vented its wrath on the beleaguered police. Up in the stands, a luckless police sergeant was strangled with his own necktie. A second officer, who went to his

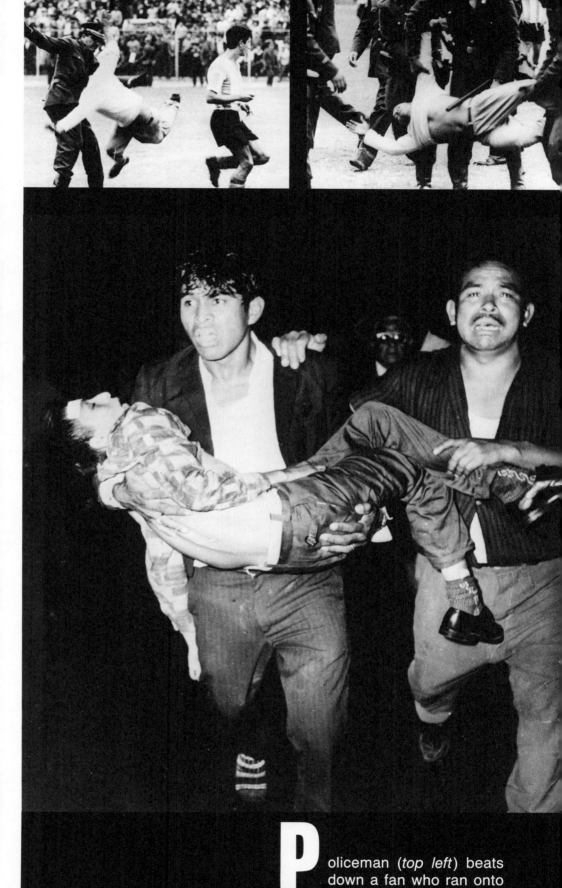

Policeman (*top left*) beats down a fan who ran onto the soccer field to assault a referee. *Top right:* Other officers carry the irate fan off the field. *Above:* An anguished father is aided by a friend as they carry away the body of his son, killed in the rioting.

rescue, was picked up by the mob and hurled from the stadium to his death on the concrete 50 feet below. Still another officer was thrown into the path of the fleeing crowd and trampled to death.

Outside the stadium, hoodlums joined the crowd. They overturned cars and buses and set them afire. They broke windows and looted stores. Reinforced police fired into the ranks of one group of rioters, killing one and wounding six.

Inside the stadium, ghouls crept among the bodies, stealing money, rings, watches and anything else of value.

As darkness drew a veil over the carnage, the madness abated. Bodies were brought out of the stadium that had become a charnel house and were laid out on the sidewalk. Some, horribly crushed, still bore the deep imprint of the gate grillwork. Others were unmarked; they had suffocated.

Bodies of men, women and children were jammed into some exits so tightly that they had to be pried apart. The injured were rushed to hospitals in ambulances and, when ambulances ran out, in commandeered taxis and cars.

Throughout the cold night, the living wandered dazedly among the dead, searching and hoping they would not find what they sought. Every now and then, a man would emit a strangled cry and sink to his knees beside the crushed body of his child.

In all, 328 men, women and children perished in those brief moments of blind panic. Another 500 were injured, many of them severely.

Outside several of the hospitals, mobs formed and chanted "revenge" and "down with the police," whom they blamed for touching off the panic.

In the glare of floodlights, police continued to remove bodies from the stadium field, now soggy from dampness and scattered with litter. Blood was splattered along the concrete ramps leading from the field.

One Lima newspaper reflected the shock felt by the nation with a headline that read: "Collective Madness."

Even the Vatican newspaper, *L'Osservatore Romano,* would comment later that partisan zeal in sports "must avoid excesses that debase human conditions."

That night, President Fernando Belaunde Terry of Peru decreed the suspension of constitutional rights for 30 days and placed the entire country under modified martial law. In restive Latin America, where a soccer game can turn into a bloody riot, the riot also can turn into revolution.

That night, too, a special detail of police spirited the hapless referee, Angel Eduardo Pazos, to the airport and the first plane for Montevideo.

Safe at home, he insisted: "I was correct in my call. There was no mistake. I called the game by the rules."

As he talked, he broke into tears.

Another distraught father clutches the limp body of his son, one of hundreds of people killed in the soccer riot. The scene was to be repeated many times in the aftermath of the tragic match.

146

# DEATH OF A GENERATION

**T**his mountain of slag towered above Aberfan for more than 50 years. Then it fell, and 144 persons—most of them children—lost their lives. *Inset:* Another view of the path of death and destruction of the coal waste landslide at Aberfan. The slide flattened houses, center, and the school, center right.

Photos by United Press International

For more than half a century, the huge slag heap at Aberfan had towered above the village, an unfriendly sight, but not an uncommon one in the grim coal mining valleys of South Wales.

Such slag heaps, known in Wales as coal tips, are an ugly feature of Britain's coal fields. The mountains of pit waste—rock, slate, dirt and fragments of coal—stand alongside the collieries, the daily dump for underground mining rubbish.

At Aberfan, a village of 5,000 persons who lived in gray stone cottages that dotted the terraced hillsides, the ugly slag heap stood 800 feet high, the sludge from 70 years of working the Merthyr Vale mine. For years, the villagers feared that one day the glowering pile might crash down on their homes. But they had learned to live with their fear.

On Friday, October 21, 1966, the 254 children at Aberfan's Pentglas Junior and Infants School had just finished prayers and were settling down for lessons. The youngsters had a special reason to be gay on this chilly, gray morning: they were just three hours away from a week's vacation. Just three hours. . . .

Checking on reports that the mountain of slag might have been undermined by earlier torrential rains, David John Evans, a maintenance man at Merthyr Vale, and another workman climbed to the top of the man-made mountain to have a look.

"Suddenly I saw the heap shifting about 300 yards away," Evans was to testify later. "Down it rumbled toward the village, disappearing into thick fog. The movement was like thunder. We could hear trees on each side being crushed to matchwood."

There was no way to warn the valley folk; a telephone line from mountain to mine had been stolen two years earlier and had not been replaced.

For the people of Aberfan, their nightmare had become reality.

The wave of soft, heavy coal sludge, an estimated two million tons of it, slid about a half a mile and engulfed the village schoolhouse and a number of nearby homes.

One awestruck witness described the scene: "This was how Pompeii died under volcanic ash." But this dark, menacing mountain didn't erupt. It split and plunged downward. Like the people of ancient Pompeii, the villagers of Aberfan rushed from their homes when they heard the rumbling.

But for many of the children of Pentglas School, there was no escape.

Pearl Crowe, wife of the proprietor of the Mackintosh Hotel directly opposite the school, said, "I was awakened soon after 9

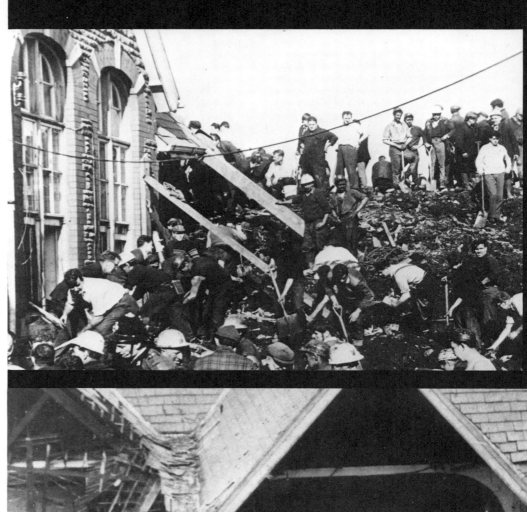

**M**iners and other rescuers (*top*) dig frantically in the ruins of Pentglas School, in Aberfan, Wales, after it was engulfed by a mountain of pit waste from a nearby mine.

**M**ore than a day later, rescue workers continued to toil in the black slime that slipped down the mountain and covered part of a school (*above*). Hundreds of miners and others pitched into the rescue effort.

**T**he Welsh mining communities have lived with tragedy for many years. But nothing more tragic than this avalanche. Here (*top left*), a victim of the landslide is removed from a school that was buried by the sludge.

**A** constable (*top right*) carries an injured child from the Pentglas School in background.

**A** police sergeant (*above*) guards pieces of clothing and other personal effects belonging to staff and children buried under the debris at Pentglas School as rescuers toiled in the chilling mist.

o'clock by the roar of the moving slag. I looked out of my bedroom window to see a black mass of waste pouring steadily on the school. Part of the school collapsed. It was terrible. For a moment I was paralyzed with shock."

Some children in classrooms on the downslope side of the voracious avalanche managed to escape through windows.

Ten-year-old Dilys Pope gave this description:

"We had just got into our class and we were talking among ourselves while waiting for the roll call. We heard a noise and then the room seemed to be flying around. The desks were falling over and the children were shouting and screaming.

"We couldn't see anything. My leg was caught in a desk and I couldn't move it and my arm was hurting. Children were lying all over the place. Our teacher was on the floor, too. His leg was caught but he managed to free himself and smashed the window to let some of us out."

Within moments of the disaster, a massive rescue effort was mobilized. Tough Welsh miners from Merthyr Vale and neighboring pits came with picks, shovels, bulldozers and tractors to search the black slime. Some looked for their own children. All around them were mothers, kneeling and weeping in grief.

Doctors, police, firemen, civil defense volunteers and hundreds of others converged on Aberfan to help in the rescue effort; some tore at the rubble until their fingernails were broken and bleeding.

"The mountain had been piling higher and higher and with a stream filtering beneath it, we knew it was always liable to shift," cried one miner. "Now it has happened, with these terrible results."

The rescuers worked into the night, eerie figures in the glare of searchlights, drifting mists and smoke from fires in the buried homes, hoping against hope that some survivors might be found. Some were. Periodically, there came a shout for silence and the hundreds of workers would listen tensely, hoping to hear a cry which would show some life existed beneath the sludge.

The body of the deputy schoolmaster was found with his arms encircling the bodies of five of his pupils. Other youngsters were found huddled over their desks. All had been suffocated by the entombing mass.

Ann Jennings, the 64-year-old headmistress of the school, was pulled out alive and taken to a hospital. Rescuers told of the incredible escape of 8-year-old Jeffrey Edwards. As the torrent of black mud surged through the school, Jeffrey's desk was flung against the wall, creating a pocket of air around him until rescued.

One woman who got into the school shortly after it was struck was Pauline Evans, 27.

I climbed through a window with a nurse," she said. "About a dozen children were screaming in one classroom which had half collapsed. We helped them out a window. In another room which was terribly damaged, we could hear a little girl.

"We could not get to her because there were other children trapped nearby and if we moved anything, it would have collapsed on

A Welsh miner takes a moment from his rescue work to survey the disaster scene at Aberfan, where 116 children and 28 adults died.

**A**n earth moving machine bores into a barrier of coal mine waste which blocks street in Aberfan. At right is part of the Pentglas School which bore the brunt of the slide.

them. So we could not rescue the little girl, who said her name was Catherine. I can't stop thinking about her."

Another rescuer, choking with sobs, said he pulled a little boy out of the rubble alive, but had to break his leg to free him.

All day long, little bodies taken from the remains of the school were carried on stretchers to a nearby chapel. There, they were laid in plain wooden coffins as bereaved parents filed in to identify them.

Prince Philip, husband of Queen Elizabeth II, donned rubber boots and trudged grim-faced through the muck. Inside the chapel, the prince saw the bodies of the children laid side by side and said, "This is dreadful, dreadful."

Prime Minister Harold Wilson walked through the disaster area with bowed head and said, "I don't think any of us can find words to describe this tragedy."

He was echoed by Glyn Williams, leader of the Welsh Miners Union. "The valleys of Wales have seen their tragedies, but never like this one."

Even as they spoke, debris being carted off by trucks contained poignant reminders of the tragedy of a few hours before—school textbooks, pieces of clothing, a broken doll, pencils and pieces of chalk.

In all, 116 children and 28 adults had perished. Almost everyone in Aberfan age 9 to 11 died.

"A generation of children has been wiped out in this village," said George Thomas, minister of state for Wales.

The National Coal Board, which operates Britain's state-owned coal industry, blamed the tragedy on abnormal rainfall.

It said in a statement: "Preliminary investigations of the tip [slag heap] slide at Merthyr Vale Colliery suggests that the recent abnormal rainfall had so permeated the tip currently in use that internal water pressure reached a strength which burst the base of the tip and movement down the mountain took place most suddenly."

Pent-up emotions of bereaved parents erupted at an inquest later. When the coroner announced that the death of one child was caused by asphyxia and multiple injuries, the victim's father shouted, "No, sir, buried alive by the National Board!"

Mothers, who said that warnings and complaints about the peril had been ignored, accused the board of "killing our children."

And the Rev. Kenneth Hays of the Zion Baptist Church, whose own son perished in Pentglas School, preached in an emotion-filled Sunday sermon: "The only appeal I would make to the National Coal Board is: don't tip any more here. Spare us that."

Parliament would be told in a few days that emergency action already had been taken to remedy a hazardous condition at three other slag dumps in Wales and that immediate inspection of 500 other such mountains had been ordered.

A lengthy government probe produced a report which laid the blame for the Aberfan disaster directly on the National Coal Board.

The report added, "The Aberfan disaster is a terrifying tale of bungling ineptitude by many men charged with tasks for which they were totally unfitted. . . ."

# CAMILLE WAS NO LADY

**T**hese are the kind of wind furies that Hurricane Camille unleashed on the Gulf Coast.

She was born off the coast of Africa. Then she made her way across the Atlantic, freshened herself with damp air in the Caribbean, and stayed briefly on the Gulf Coast of the United States.

But before she breathed her last, far inland, Hurricane Camille had got the reputation as the worst disaster ever to hit the nation, a "once-in-a-lifetime hurricane."

Before her destructive path faded, Camille had left more than 200 persons dead, damage across the South reckoned at $1.5 billion and tens of thousands of families homeless.

In terms of lost lives, the country had witnessed worse storms in earlier days. A 1900 hurricane which struck the Texas coast had left between 5,000 and 8,000 dead at Galveston. And in 1938, a hurricane which struck Long Island and lower New England killed more than 600 people.

However, no other storm had left such wide-ranging destruction and desolation as did Camille in that summer of 1969.

Mississippi, whose coastline was described as looking "like Hiroshima after the atom bomb," counted at least 132 dead. Other deaths were recorded in Louisiana and Virginia; West Virginia, hard hit by floods created by Camille's dying gasp over Appalachia, listed 111 dead.

The actual number of dead probably will never be known. Reconnaissance pilots, flying over the Gulf Coast days after Camille passed, reported sighting clusters of bodies which had been swept out to sea by incredible tides.

By 9:40 A.M., Sunday, August 17, Camille was reported 200 miles south of New Orleans. Weather forecasters were all but sure she would smash into the Florida Panhandle.

But whipping the Gulf of Mexico into an angry white froth, Camille instead invaded the marshy coast of Louisiana that afternoon, sliced across the state's oil-rich underbelly, then raged through Venice and other hamlets in the Mississippi River delta as she moved north. All during that grim morning, as radio stations continually announced weather bulletins, a stream of traffic had choked the highways leading out of New Orleans. Only later was it clear that the storm center had veered 60 miles east of the city.

Water rose late in the day in fringe areas of New Orleans and some families were evacuated. Dr. Robert Simpson of the National Hurricane Center in Miami said that had Camille held her course toward the city the death toll could have reached 50,000.

While skirting the heavily populated lower course of the Mississippi, the storm stirred up violent tides that surged up the big river. A wall of water smashed over the 15-foot levee at Buras, Louisiana, and submerged the town in 12- to 15-foot waters. A few Civil Defense workers and others who

**T**he toll bridge on U.S. Highway 90 at Bay St. Louis, Mississippi, is almost hidden under a mass of lumber and debris left by Camille.

**T**he freighter *Silver Hawk,* beached at Gulfport by Hurricane Camille, appears to be adrift on a sea of debris. She was one of two cargo vessels run aground by the 200-mile-an-hour winds.

**C**amille left her footprint along this section of Highway 90 at Bay St. Louis, Mississippi.

**A**n elderly woman patient from Bay St. Louis Hospital is lifted by a Coast Guardsman for evacuation to New Orleans.

remained in the stricken town found an uneasy refuge on the second floor of a school building.

Throughout the low delta area of Louisiana's Plaquemines Parish, martial law was imposed and deputies with shotguns turned back residents seeking to check on their homes. Of one hard-hit area, officials said, "There are no homes there. There are no grocery stores. Nothing, period. A few telephone poles, tugs in the marsh, houses in the marsh—or parts of them." One Plaquemines official lashed himself to a building and rode out the storm. He said he felt throughout that long black night that he wouldn't survive.

It wasn't until sunrise on the following day that Camille's full devastation became known. Little remained wherever she had struck. Resort towns such as Pass Christian, Mississippi, and nearby Waveland had all but vanished. The bustling vacation centers of Biloxi and Gulfport were hard hit.

"The wind is blowing rocks," reported a deputy from Gulfport. "There's a boat out in the parking lot here, and we're three blocks from the harbor!"

Camille's fury seemed indomitable. The six-story Hancock Bank Building, a possible shield for Pass Christian's tiny business district, disappeared. Only its vault remained.

Winds estimated at well over 200 miles an hour lifted the railroad tracks off of the Louisville and Nashville trestle across the Bay of St. Louis, and communication systems were obliterated.

At first, searchers found only a few bodies. Then the toll rose rapidly.

At Pass Christian, a community of 4,000, the dead were draped across tree limbs, pinned beneath the eaves of crushed houses, and sprawled under bushes. A monstrous tidal wave, its height estimated at 20 feet, washed over the resort. Graves in the town's tiny cemetery were opened by the swamping water and newly buried caskets were torn open.

In Pass Christian Isles, Mary and Bill Gatipan had put 20 years' savings into their home. When they returned a few days after the storm, Mrs. Gatipan found a new stove on the front lawn. The roof over their 30-foot veranda was found 100 feet away, its concrete pillars still attached. Pieces of the living room dangled from the branches of trees more than a block away.

Similar scenes were duplicated a hundredfold. Dr. Walter Peat had sent his wife to Miami to visit a daughter a few days before the storm. But Peat and his son, Buzz, decided to remain in Pass Christian. Their house crumbled when wind and water slammed into it. Father and son grabbed a section of masonry still standing and clung to it all night. They were found alive, 40 feet above ground, jammed between a tree branch and the remaining wall of another building.

The storm's concentrated fury stretched from the Louisiana coast to Pascagoula, just west of Mobile, Alabama. Camille swept fashionable motel cabins from the beach near Biloxi, and restaurants that had lined the oceanfront disappeared.

At Pascagoula, a new kind of terror ap-

peared. Snakes crawled out of the marshes to invade the town. Merle Palmer, a state senator, said, "We had to organize to fight them."

And Mrs. Ann Mansfield, another resident, said, "There were hundreds, I mean hundreds, of black water moccasins and cottonmouths in the water in my mother's backyard."

Caring for the dead and injured left in Camille's swath of destruction became a herculean task. Bodies had to be tagged and sent to temporary morgues. More than 75,000 families along the storm's lengthy route suffered heavy losses. Food and shelter, of some kind, had to be found for them. The Red Cross and Salvation Army established temporary kitchens and housing areas.

Why was the death toll so high? Weather Bureau advisories all day Sunday had warned that the storm was a killer and had urged all persons in Camille's path to evacuate.

"The people just wouldn't get out," said Gulfport Mayor Philip Shaw. "It's human nature to think that the safest place is their home. If the people had believed us, there wouldn't have been anybody in town."

There had been hurricanes before to test the strength of the Gulf Coast. A big one that roared through in 1947 had left her scars. There had been Betsy in 1965, then Inez in 1966, and Beulah which struck the following year. But none matched Camille.

She had left a shambles of the Gulf Coast, but her destructive career had not ended. She knifed deeper inland, her winds tempered to gale strength; but her heavy rains touched off life-taking flash floods in West Virginia and Virginia.

Roaring streams in West Virginia drowned many, wrecked homes, washed out roads and smashed bridges. An Army engineer said the concentration of rain—as much as 10 inches in a few hours—brought on flooding "just as if you'd try to pour a bucket of water into a thimble."

And in Virginia, rivers flowing down the side of the Blue Ridge Mountains swept through villages and towns.

Massies Mill, a tiny community of only 125, was ruined by the Tye River and, for two days, reachable only by helicopter. As the flood waters rose, Mrs. B. W. Ponton, a 70-year-old, moved to the second story of her home. The flood waters finally stopped at the eighth step of the staircase.

By the time some semblance of normalcy began to return to the Gulf Coast, the remains of Camille were far out in the Atlantic. But for many years to come, her scars would remain.

**T**his woman, on right in top photo, found a little joy among the devastation as her 2-month-old son was baptized amid the ruins of St. Thomas Catholic Church. The child is held by his godparents.

**F**our months after Hurricane Camille roared through her home, Shirley Carpenter hung a Christmas wreath on the front door. Mrs. Carpenter, who moved into a nearby trailer, used the desolate setting as a Christmas card to send her friends.

**T**his youngster found he had nothing to come back to five days after Hurricane Camille swept through Buras, Louisiana. He and many thousands found their homes reduced to kindling by the destructive winds.

**W**orkers at a morgue in Gulfport, Mississippi, try to identify some of the victims of Hurricane Camille.

# A KILLING WINTER

Photo by United Press International

**T**he village of Val d'Isère, where an avalanche of snow and ice roared down a mountain, to the right out of view, and killed 39 persons, mostly young skiers.

SWITZ.

Plateau d'Assy
Passy ✠ **Avalanche**
Chamonix

F  R  A  N  C  E

FRANCE

Mont
Blanc

I  T  A  L  Y

Little
St. Bernard
Pass

Bourg St-Maurice

Ste-Foy

Isère

Tignes
Le
Dôme

Val d'Isère ✠
**Avalanche**

0                    10 Miles

The winter of 1969–70 had been an unusually long one in the French Alps, with some of the heaviest snowfalls in memory.

On the morning of February 10, 1970, the group of young holiday-goers, seated around the breakfast tables at Val d'Isère could not have cared less about how much snow had fallen in past storms. Their only concern was in a new storm which at that time threatened their ski activity.

"There was a gay, happy atmosphere at the dining tables," recalled Jean-Charles Loos. "We were talking about where we would go skiing."

Then the chatter stopped. "There was this rumbling sound," said the 25-year-old Loos. "The noise became deafening. I realized it was an avalanche. I just had time to dive against the wall for protection. Then a great wall of snow burst through the door and hit me. I was submerged and remember no more until I woke up in a neighboring house." Loos had suffered head and hip injuries. For many of his friends and associates, fate was less kind.

Loosened by up to 60-mile-an-hour winds of a wild French alpine blizzard, tons of snow thundered a half mile down the south slope of the 7,000-foot crest of Le Dôme which overlooks the famous winter resort.

The mass of snow which came down from Le Dôme jumped a national highway, a river, crushed two garages and ripped the roof off a hotel before crashing like a runaway locomotive through the doors and bay windows of the ski camp's dining room.

Survivors told of the terrible roar of the deadly avalanche, which experts estimated had hit 120 miles an hour before piling into the resort like a giant sledgehammer.

The white fury left 39 persons dead and 31 injured in what was then considered one of Europe's worst single avalanche disasters of the century.

The dining room was buried and few of the 30 or so eating there escaped alive. The walls were spattered with the blood from bodies crushed against a wall under the pressure from the slide.

Most of the dead and injured were young people enjoying a low-cost ski vacation at the Union of Fresh Air Centers. Of the 194 guests, many were French postal and railway workers. There were about 20 Belgians and six West Germans staying at the camp's hostel.

Some bodies, including those of ski trail workers going to their jobs, were hurled high in the air. The slide's 100-yard front picked up automobiles and carried them like

**R**oute taken by the Plateau d'Assy avalanche (*top right*). A sudden thaw had dislodged snow and rock high on the 6,000-foot slope. *Right:* Inside the youth hostel where many skiers lost their lives when the avalanche thundered into the building.

**L**ittle more than two months later, and not too far from Val d'Isère, an avalanche of snow and rock again swept over a tuburcular sanatorium at Plateau d'Assy (*above*). It killed 72, most of them boys under 15 years of age. *Left:* The Union of Fresh Air Center after the avalanche swept through. Most of the victims had just sat down to breakfast when the tragedy occurred.

matchwood for quite some distance.

Twenty-two-year-old Chantal Demur said she was buried for about two hours in a pocket of air under the snow before she was dug out.

And Benoit Miko, a 21-year-old from Brussels, said he was caught on the hostel stairway when the avalanche struck "with a frightening noise," sweeping him along a corridor and out a window.

"I found myself outside lying in the snow," Miko said. "My ears were still filled with the terrible sound of the avalanche. My arm was bleeding, and I wandered in a daze into a hotel opposite and asked them to bind me up."

Miko said that breakfast was just about over and had the avalanche struck about five minutes later, the dining room would have been empty.

"I was sure lucky," Miko said. "God, was I lucky."

Miko said he and other survivors returned to the dining room to find metal tables twisted into so much junk. Even a stove in the kitchen had been cut in half by the force of the slide. Then, using plates and their bare hands, they began digging for survivors.

Tourists joined police and army troops in the rescue effort. Electronic sounding devices were used in the search for bodies buried under the tons of snow.

Rescue work went on despite blizzard conditions and near-zero visibility. Natives of Val d'Isère, home of French ski champions Jean-Claude Killy and Marielle and Christine Goitschel, called the storm the worst they could ever remember.

Jacques Sifferlen, a student who narrowly missed death in the snowslide, said he joined rescue efforts, but a lot of victims were stuck in the snow "like concrete."

Worsening weather continued to hamper rescue efforts. Between the resort and Bourg-Saint-Maurice in the valley, drifting snow continued to cover the road. Police blocked it to all but emergency traffic and sent a snowplow through to lead each ambulance convoy.

Two days later, a convoy of seven black vans, led by snowplows and military vehicles, reached Val d'Isère. They carried coffins for the dead.

The storm continued unabated, giving rise to fears of new snowslides. As 40- to 50-mile-an-hour winds howled through the valley and snow continued to accumulate, six hotels and a youth hostel were evacuated in the ski center.

Avalanches rumbled during the day at three points along the road between Val d'Isère and Bourg-Saint-Maurice, where rescue efforts were being coordinated. A fourth slide hit a convoy of vehicles leaving Bourg-Saint-Maurice, but fortunately no one was injured.

Even as rescue attempts were underway, controversy erupted as to whether the area, because of possible danger of snowslides, should not have been closed earlier to tourists.

The resort's security chief, Jacques Jouve, said there was nothing to indicate danger on Le Dôme.

Jacques Boule, a departmental official, said that an avalanche the previous week at Tignes, five miles from Val d'Isère, had killed four persons, making the catastrophe at Val d'Isère "forewarned."

"Val d'Isère and Tignes," he said, "live under the incessant threat of avalanches and the few efforts made to take steps to head off a possible incident were minimal in relation to the risk."

But if the French counted Val d'Isère as the worst avalanche of the century, they had only to wait two months—until April 16—for a slide of more tragic dimensions.

Forty miles away from Val d'Isère, tons of mud, rock and snow, 600 feet wide and 60 feet high, swept over an alpine sanatorium on the Plateau d'Assy, killing 72 persons, most of them tubercular boys being nursed back to health.

French Health Minister Robert Boulin said the death toll was the highest ever recorded for an avalanche in Europe.

Government avalanche experts said the slide was triggered by a sudden thaw which dislodged a layer of snow high on the 6,000-foot slope which looms above the children's sanatorium.

As the avalanche sped downward, it gathered earth, rocks and trees, then roared across the plateau where the hospital stood. It swept away the concrete dormitories where 55 boys—almost all 15 years of age or younger—lay sleeping, and crumpled a chalet housing hospital personnel. It then glanced off the wing of another building where 130 patients and 70 medical workers were lodged.

One witness recalled that the slide "moved at an incredible speed and carried the dormitories away like pieces of straw."

Ernest Gras, a 60-year-old chauffeur, was in bed reading a detective story during the early morning hours when "there came a giant boom. It was like a huge cannon being fired."

Gras dressed quickly and went outside where he helped evacuate a girls' wing that had been touched by the edge of the slide. But he could not reach the boys.

"All the paths were blocked by rocks. There was nothing we could do," he said. "It was almost pitch dark except for a little moonlight and now there was dead silence."

Another survivor spoke of the terrifying sound and speed of the slide, of futile attempts to grope through mounds of debris.

"I heard cries for help. I didn't know where to go. I tried in vain to work myself into the wreckage of the nurses' chalet. A little farther on I met a nun. She was injured. She ran away crying out. After about five minutes everything was quiet. . . ."

Contractors sent earthmoving equipment to the site to help uncover the wreckage. Dogs trained to find buried victims were pressed into service.

After more than 18 hours of digging, rescue teams were able to recover only 19 torn bodies from the shattered ruins. It would be many more days before all the victims were found.

Minister Boulin, who flew from Paris for an inspection of the disaster scene, said the avalanche was "as unforeseen as an earthquake."

He dismissed complaints from local residents that a minor avalanche about two weeks earlier should have served as a warning signal. That slide reached the sanatorium but didn't damage it.

Boulin said that if there had been any doubt, the children would have been evacuated immediately.

He said experts had decided there was nothing alarming and that they found no indications of possible larger slides to follow.

Photo by United Press International

Rescuers use long sticks to probe through snow and ice in their effort to find avalanche victims.

# THE DAY THE MOUNTAIN FELL

**C**araz, another city in Huaylas Valley, lies shattered from earthquake damage. Scores died under the rubble. *Inset:* The north peak of Mt. Huascarán, the source of the massive ice and rock avalanche that buried the towns of Yungay and Ranrahirca, Peru. Slide started from part of peak in shadow.

Photo by United Press International

ECUADOR

PERU

Pacific Ocean

Lima

Pacific Ocean

Chimbote

Caraz

Avalanche

Yungay

Ranrahirca

Mt. Huascarán

Carhuaz

Casma

ANCASH

Santa R.

Earthquake Destruction

Huaraz

20 Miles

Rivers rise before the floods flow; storm clouds herald the lightning bolt. Conference and disagreement precede the first shots of war; and the tornado's telltale funnel warns of the devastation to come.

But the sudden upheaval of the earth itself is perhaps the most tragic of all disasters because it is, many times, so totally unpredictable.

It was May 31, 1970, a cool, bright day, high in the Peruvian Andes, in an isolated valley known as Callejón de Huaylas.

It was just a little shake at first. Peru had registered some 1,500 tremors yearly, most of them so slight that few paid them even scant notice.

But within seconds, this one had announced itself as a killer. It was to last an agonizing 40 seconds, rising in intensity until buildings crumbled and shivering mountains sent walls of earth and rock hurtling down on doomed villages below.

The epicenter of the earthquake was 12 miles off the port of Chimbote, but the full fury of the quake was unleashed 100 miles eastward, in Huaylas Valley.

One of the cities in the 80-mile valley was Yungay, a clean, neat community of about 4,000 persons, largely of Indian blood. It nestled in a flat area between the Santa River and the foothills of Mt. Huascarán, a 22,205-foot peak perpetually covered with snow and glaciers.

On that bright, sunny Sunday afternoon, many people were crowded around radio sets, listening to an important soccer game at the Julet Rimet tournament in Mexico City. A number of other people had gone to the city cemetery to place flowers at the feet of the typical Latin burial crypts which stair-stepped upward and around a small promontory. At the top of the promontory stood a statue of Christ, his arms outstretched toward the city.

Some of the people were kneeling, praying at the feet of the white marble statue, when suddenly the ground began quivering. They exchanged glances nervously and whispered, "Tremor," then paused in silence, waiting for the movement to subside.

It didn't. Instead, the shaking increased rapidly, violently, and soon the ground was heaving. A terrible noise rocketed through the valley, bouncing off the mountains which framed it.

Screams of "terremoto" were heard— "earthquake." And this is what they called a "vertical" quake, terrible up and down motions of the earth, instead of the more frequently experienced side-to-side shaking.

A few miles away, on a hill overlooking the city, several hundred children sat watching a circus. Suddenly, as the ground started to shake, they became hysterical, screaming for their parents and running for home.

Then, as they and the people in the cemetery watched in horror, a huge slice of Mt. Huascaran split away and began slipping, sliding, grinding downhill. It picked up speed steadily until it was roaring downward at a speed estimated at 140 miles an hour.

The gigantic mass of thousands of tons of rock, earth, mud, snow and ice slammed against a small ridge at the foot of the mountain. Yungayans always had thought the ridge would protect them from avalanches as it had

eight years earlier when a slide wiped out the neighboring city of Ranrahirca.

But this time Yungay was not to escape. The mass roared up and across the ridge, then down and over Yungay.

It smashed into the area approximately four minutes after the first rumbles of the quake had been felt, obliterating a city, its men, women and children, its records, its pets and its schools.

Spared were those who stood amid the twisted ruins of the cemetery, where many coffins hung grotesquely from their niches in adobe walls; those who had attended the circus; and the tops of five palm trees which grew in the city square. And the white marble statue of Christ.

Everything else lay beneath as much as 30 feet of mud, rock and earth.

A mile or so away, separated by a wooded hill, was the rebuilt city of Ranrahirca. This time the avalanche was so massive that it divided higher up on Mt. Huascarán, part of it sweeping down on Yungay and the remainder destroying Ranrahirca, killing some of those who had survived the 1962 avalanche.

The wall of water, rocks and mud had rushed across both cities with such speed and fury that it bridged the Santa River and splashed upward against the steep mountain walls on the valley's far side.

At the head of Callejón de Huaylas sat the city of Huaraz, capital of Ancash State, often called "The Switzerland of Peru."

Huaraz, the valley's commercial center, boasted movies, hotels, gas stations, a hospital and the area's police headquarters.

Unfortunately, Huaraz had extremely narrow streets, barely wide enough to accommodate an automobile. Most of the homes were of two stories but were of mud and brick construction covered with plaster and paint. Lacking concrete or reinforcing steel, virtually every building crumbled under the incredible power of the quake.

The city was reduced to a nearly level layer of rubble. Half of the town's 12,000 residents were killed. People who ran into the streets to escape the danger of crumbling homes, found only death from toppling walls. Automobiles were crushed into scrap metal piles only 18 inches high.

And two American Peace Corps girls who rushed into the streets died with the Peruvians they had come to help. Both were later buried in the Huaraz cemetery by fellow volunteers.

In the Peruvian capital of Lima, meanwhile, the quake had caused only five deaths, some minor damage and immense fear. But Lima knew nothing of the far greater destruction and death 200 miles to the north. Communications, never very good, had been destroyed. Eventually, a few plaintive calls for help filtered in by amateur radio, especially from Chimbote.

Since the Peruvian Seismic Institute didn't function on Sunday, it was word from the United States that finally gave Peruvian officials the epicenter's location and indicated the likely destruction in the north. But roads to Chimbote were blocked and its airstrip was knocked out. President Juan Velasco and his top aides had to take a naval cruiser for the night-long trip to Chimbote.

The death toll mounted slowly at first, reaching perhaps 1,000 by mid-Monday. Then, as information began to trickle out of stricken Huaylas Valley, the full, stark reality of the quake's magnitude unfolded.

The fatality figure was, almost reluctantly, placed at 30,000! A few days later it was revised upward to 50,000. Some speculate that as many as 80,000 perished. But no one can know for certain. Thousands were to die from their injuries and lack of immediate medical attention. Officials calculated that up to one million were made homeless.

When the extent of death and damage became known, Peru's friends hastened to her aid. Chileans, veterans of many disastrous quakes, were the first to respond, with planeloads of supplies, medical teams, shiploads of food, blankets, a field hospital and medical supplies.

The United States launched a multi-million-dollar relief program. Helicopters were rushed to Peru in giant air transports, along with medical-surgical teams, tons of food, water and medical supplies. A score of other nations from as far away as Australia and Scandinavia sent planeloads of relief supplies. Even Communist Cuba, which had no diplomatic relations with Peru, sent doctors, blood plasma, medicine—and even some articles stamped "U.S. Army."

To deliver all this to the injuired, hungry and homeless, helicopter and airplane pilots of several nations braved dangerous altitudes, narrow valleys and treacherous wind currents. Several fliers gave their lives during the rescue operation.

The First Lady of the United States, Pat Nixon, flew to Peru on one of the jet transports loaded with relief items. She and President Velasco's wife flew to the Huaylas Valley disaster area to walk through the rubble and talk to survivors.

The massive relief operation began a long and arduous road to recovery. But the survivors would never forget in their lifetime that fateful Sunday—the day of "terremoto."

Statue of Christ stands undamaged in cemetery overlooking Yungay, Peru. The statue, along with four palm trees and parts of burial crypts, were all that remained of town after the earthquake and avalanche of 1970.

An overturned bus, atop a pile of debris, stands mutely against the sky in what was once the center of the village of Yungay, now buried under 15 feet of mud and rock.

Photo by United Press International

The stench of the dead hung heavy over the city of Huaraz two weeks after

Photo by United Press International

**E**ight years earlier, the town of Ranrahirca suffered another avalanche. Here, the villagers try to identify their dead from that disaster.

**I**n the city of Chimbote, a mother cradles her injured child while awaiting evacuation. The quake was the worst in Peruvian history and one of the worst ever recorded in South America.

# FAMINE IN THE SUB-SAHARA

**V**illages of graves dot the arid plains of Wollo Province in Eastern Ethiopia. Thousands died of hunger in Sub-Sahara Africa in the wake of one of the worst droughts in history.

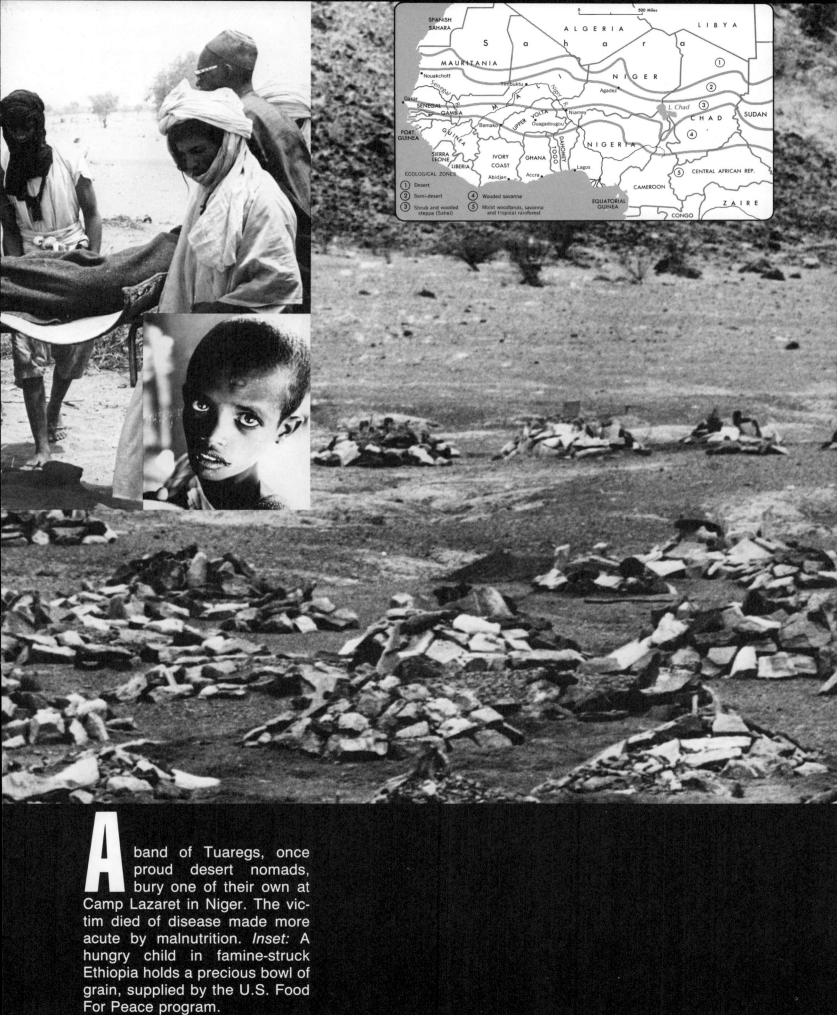

**A** band of Tuaregs, once proud desert nomads, bury one of their own at Camp Lazaret in Niger. The victim died of disease made more acute by malnutrition. *Inset:* A hungry child in famine-struck Ethiopia holds a precious bowl of grain, supplied by the U.S. Food For Peace program.

Photo courtesy of the United Nations

Starving young victims of drought and famine in Moyali, a rural village of Ethiopia. Tens of thousands perished not only of malnutrition but disease as well.

Thomas Malthus, an 18th-century English parson and economist, concluded 200 years ago that unless war and disease intervened to diminish excessive population, man would be consigned to starvation.

His grim conclusion was based on his belief then that the world's food supply just could not keep up with the ever-growing population.

In one part of the world during the 1970s, a searing drought gave Malthus' prophecy a horrendous reality.

Graves and the sun-bleached bones of dead cattle littered the parched southern rim of the Sahara Desert in an arc from sand-swept Mauritania and Senegal on the western bulge of Africa through land-locked Mali, Upper Volta, Niger and Chad to Ethiopia.

By 1974, the impact of five years of little rain in a region where water is more precious than gold had struck sub-Saharan Africa a crippling blow.

West Africa's two great waterways—the Senegal and Niger rivers—dropped to the lowest level farmers could remember in more than half a century. And placid Lake Chad, which laps the shores of Niger, Chad, Cameroon and Nigeria in the heart of Africa, shrank to a fraction of its normal dry season size of 4,000 square miles.

In the semi-desert wilderness just below the Sahara the ground, baked by the 120-degree heat, hardened and cracked. The far-flung desert water holes, life-giving rest stops for Saharan nomads, dried up.

Further south, meager crops of millet and sorghum, food staples of Africa, withered and died under the sun's searing rays. Across the bleak shrub and sparsely wooded steppe known as the *Sahel*—a vast area of more than 2.5 million miles—hundreds of thousands of subsistence farmers and nomads began fleeing the specter of famine.

They trudged south, abandoning the dustbowl conditions of the north for the lusher lands of the coastal states. They streamed into Senegal, Ivory Coast, Ghana and Nigeria. Peasant herdsmen desperately seeking food for their starved animals cut down tree branches across West Africa's savanna belt.

Hunger drove thousands of farmers to eat seeds stockpiled for planting, leaving virtually nothing to plant for future harvests. Tens of thousands of sheep, cattle and goats perished in the long march to the south.

The full human and economic toll in an area embracing some of the world's poorest, most backward nations was without reckoning. For countries where more than 75 per cent of the people had to scrape a meager living off the land in the best of times, it was a major catastrophe.

The white skeletons of man and beast in the cinnamon sand, the dusty river banks, the burned-out fields, and the deserted mud-hut villages marked one of the worst ecological and human disasters ever to hit the globe.

Thousands of persons—no one knew exactly how many—died in 1973 and 1974 of starvation and disease, especially cholera and measles, made more virulent by acute malnutrition.

Photo courtesy of the United Nations

**A**t Tanut, Niger, these women (*top*) waited for several hours in the hope of obtaining a few kilos of millet or sorghum to enable them to subsist for a few more days. They traveled a long distance to this village seeking food.

**T**hey lined up for food, when and where they could find it. Above, villagers of Bume, Ethiopia, found it at a food distribution center set up by the government with the help of UN emergency supplies.

The children succumbed first to the gnawing hunger. Then it was the turn of the old, the sick and the weak. One 1973 estimate put the death toll at more than 100,000 in West Africa and between 50,000 and 100,000 in Ethiopia.

In the mass migration of refugees, countless thousands of hungry men, women and children abandoned their ancestral homes for the promise of survival further south. Some made it; others died from the effort. Many found new homes in sprawling refugee camps that sprouted on the fringes of remote settlements and the larger towns.

Legendary desert outposts like Timbuktu in Mali and Agadez in Niger, flourishing trade centers supplied by richly laden camel caravans in centuries past, took on a grim new identity as emergency relief distribution points.

But it was the nomads, particularly the Tuaregs, the famed "blue men" of the Sahara, who were among the hardest hit. While the farmers could hope to return to the soil and replant their crops, the nomads, entirely dependent on their herds for survival, lost everything.

For them the solution to a food shortage a century earlier had been bloody, effective and quick. Mounted on bellowing camels, the tough Tuareg warriors would swoop down on the black farmers to the south, sacking granaries and looting villages. Now, the fierce Tuaregs sat in squalid refugee camps living on handouts of food from abroad.

The United Nations Food and Agriculture Organization (FAO) calculated that more than 3.5 million cattle were wiped out in 1973 in the six West African countries.

There were no precise figures for the millions of goats, sheep and camels also wiped out. But in the Agadez region which embraces the northern half of Niger—an area larger than all of France—officials estimated that all the sheep, 95 per cent of the cattle, 70 per cent of the donkeys, half the camels and a third of the goat herds had perished.

"We are like birds without wings," mourned a Tuareg refugee who sat in a camp just outside Niamey, the capital of Niger.

By the close of 1974, human deaths already were reckoned at about half a million in the Sahel and the prospect of death by starvation faced tens of thousands more.

**T**he faces of hunger and despair. Two women victims of the Northwest Africa drought and famine sit in a camp in Upper Volta.

A catastrophe of even greater dimensions was blunted somewhat by a massive international relief operation that kept millions alive. More than a million tons of food grains were pumped into the region. In the years 1973–1974 the multinational emergency effort channeled $5.6 million through a special UNICEF relief and rehabilitation program.

Relief supplies came by ship to the coastal ports of West Africa and were transported by truck, barge, train and camel throughout the drought-ravaged regions. Life-saving airlifts carried food to starving thousands in the more remote areas cut off from the rest of the world.

But even the relief operations found themselves plagued by everything from anti-government rebels in Chad to deep-rooted African pride. There also were complaints of corruption, the soaring cost of transport and tribal discrimination in food distribution. A lack of paved roads, poor communications and shortages of fuel also frustrated relief efforts.

As another dry "rainy season" ended in late 1973 and the new year dawned, it became increasingly clear that the drought, like an invisible blight, was spreading south. It struck crops and livestock in several West African coastal nations including Gambia, Guinea, Ivory Coast and Nigeria. Cameroon, Kenya and Tanzania also felt the impact of the drought.

UN Secretary-General Kurt Waldheim, after a tour of the region in early 1974, described the crisis as "incredible . . . a very tragic situation." Clearly alarmed by the unrelenting advance of the drought, Waldheim warned that some of the worst-hit nations faced "being wiped off the map" within the next decade.

But in the summer of 1974, the rains finally came—and in near-normal amounts for the first time in more than five years.

Despite the rains, however, the future of the region remained bleak.

Relief experts said millions of famished Africans would have to be supported with outside food supplies for years to avert starvation. Poor crop rotation, inadequate irrigation, and overgrazing of land in marginally productive areas even in the best of times would be unable to support their populations.

Thousands upon thousands of cattle died in the drought zone of Northwest Africa, including this stretch of parched land (*top*) in the interior of Senegal. *Right:* Starving villagers of Bume, Ethiopia, gathered at a government food distribution center for emergency supplies provided by various governments and UN agencies.

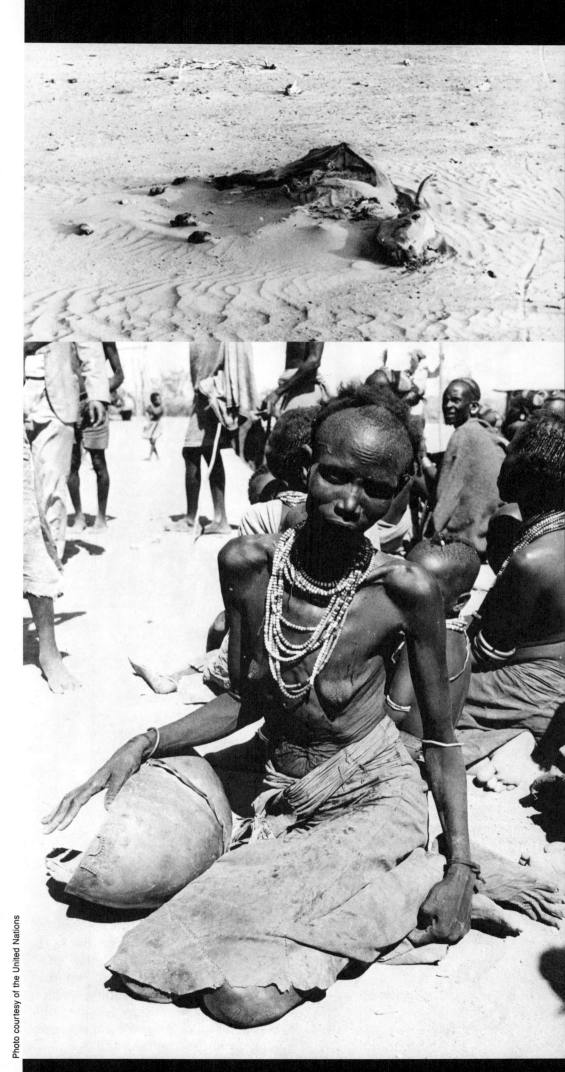

Photo courtesy of the United Nations

# THE "TOWERING INFERNO"– BRAZIL STYLE

**F**lames surged upward through the top floors of the Crefisul Investment Bank Building in downtown São Paulo, Brazil, trapping office workers on window ledges, balconies and the roofs. The towering inferno claimed 179 lives.

BRAZIL

PARAGUAY

Brasília

São
Paulo

**Skyscraper
Fire** ✠

Rio de
Janeiro

0 ___ 400 Miles

This grim, close-up photograph catches a man leaping to his death from one of the upper floors of a São Paulo skyscraper. A number of victims jumped to escape the searing flames and choking smoke.

A light rain was falling and a number of employees already had arrived for work at the Crefisul Investment Bank Building in downtown São Paulo, Brazil, on the morning of February 1, 1974. The Crefisul was one of Brazil's largest investment and savings banks.

On the 12th floor of the 25-floor skyscraper, defective wiring that fed several ceiling lamps and air conditioners sparked a small blaze and, within minutes, the building was turned into a deadly furnace of heat, smoke and flames.

The flames surged upward through the top 14 floors of the bank building, trapping office workers on window ledges, small balconies and on the twin roofs.

Drawn by the screams of many sirens and a forbidding dark column of smoke, thousands of persons crowded into the area surrounding the towering inferno.

They stood there helplessly as person after person trapped in the building leaped to their deaths in a futile attempt to escape the flames.

Neusa de Souza, a nurse for more than 20 years, sobbed, "I never saw anything like this in my life. The people are dying and we can't do anything."

Before the orange flames were brought under control, 188 of the more than 500 persons inside had perished or suffered fatal injuries—many from panic.

When some of the trapped victims jumped to their deaths in desperation, the helpless crowd below tried to shout encouragement to those remaining: "No, don't jump," "Wait for help" and "The fire is dying," the crowd cried.

Several sheets, on which the words "Calm" and "Danger is past" were scrawled, were held on the street for the people in the burning building to see.

As the fire raged out of control, fed by drafts shooting up an unprotected stairwell which acted as a chimney, bodies could be seen at the foot of the skyscraper, crumpled amid broken glass and other debris.

Sergeant Alicio Zanca of the State Military Police Force, said, "I saw several bodies being picked up. The bottoms of their feet were burned. That made them desperate."

At least two falling persons landed on a crowded ladder, injuring others as they were being rescued. One fire official said many became desperate and jumped when they saw that fire ladders would be unable to reach them.

Other victims perished inside the building, overcome by dense smoke and heat. In one rest room, rescuers found eight dead women.

The dead included two American executives on loan to Crefisul from the affili-

**A**mbulances, lower left, line up before the burned out bank building as they await to take fire victims to nearby morgues for identification.

**S**ome Air Force helicopters were able to land on the roof to begin ferrying survivors of the fire to safety.

**A**lthough the heat on the roof was intense, many who had fled to the roof were able to escape.

**I**nvestigators go through rubble in the aftermath of the bank building fire, which was blamed on defective wiring.

ated First National City Bank of New York.

Bank officials said several persons died of heart attacks, including some young secretaries whose unburned bodies were found on one of the roofs.

Rudolpho Manfredo, Jr., 20, was one of the 80 persons who sought refuge on one of the roofs and survived.

On his roof, he said, the heat was intense. But many survived. On the other roof, no one escaped.

As firemen tried desperately to curb the flames, people on the upper floors waved frantically at small helicopters that were unable to rescue them because of the heat, smoke and lack of a landing pad. As the fire died down, larger Air Force helicopters arrived and, hovering just above the roof, began ferrying survivors to safety.

Sergeant Augusto Carlos Cassanico of the State Police was the first rescue worker to land on the roof by chopper. His mission was to calm survivors and do whatever possible for the injured.

Cassanico said he found one severely burned young woman, who begged him, "Don't let me die, don't let me die." But she did.

"Her voice was so suffering that I started crying," said the veteran sergeant. "I applied artificial respiration, trying to revive her, but it was impossible."

As firemen on the ground sprayed jets of water into the roaring flames, rescue workers brought a number of survivors down ladders. Some people trapped on upper balconies tried to lower themselves on makeshift curtain ropes to ladders which reached only midway up the building.

About 300 survivors and injured rescue workers were treated in hospitals, and 15 firemen suffered from smoke inhalation.

And in a nearby morgue, scores of victims lay waiting for identification by grieving relatives.

The bank reopened the week after the

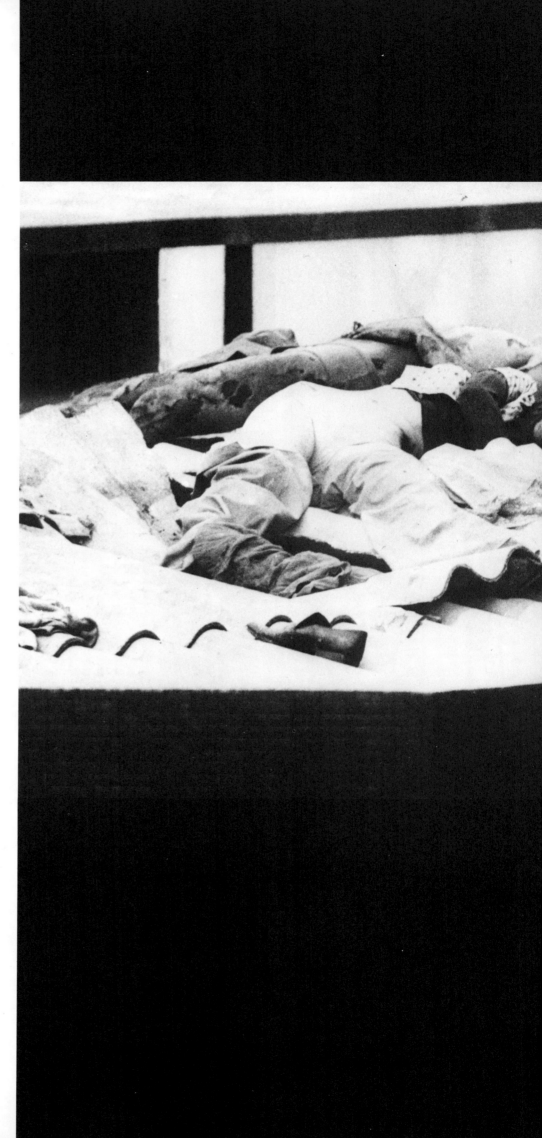

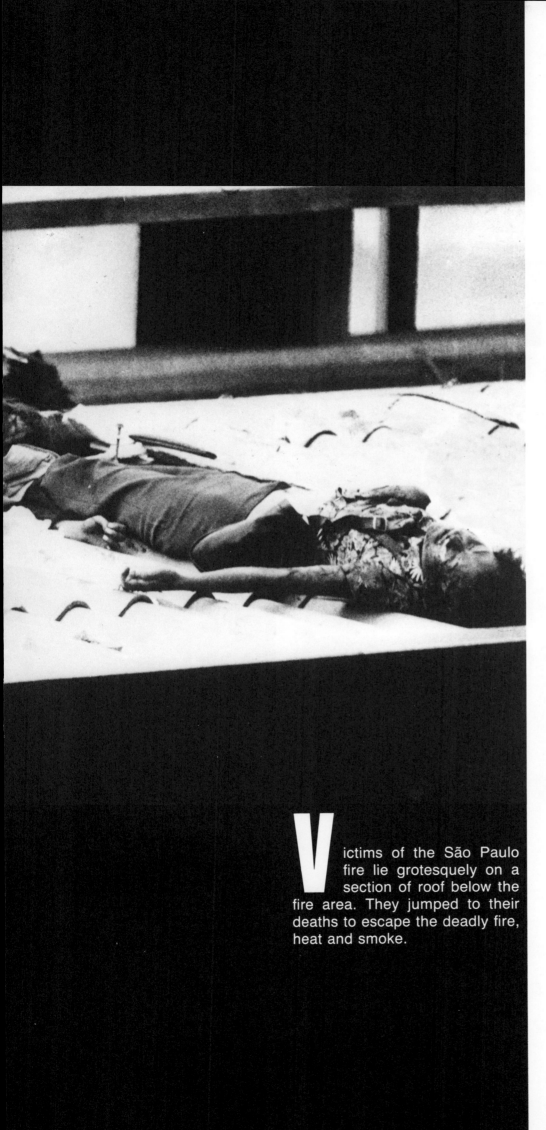

**V**ictims of the São Paulo fire lie grotesquely on a section of roof below the fire area. They jumped to their deaths to escape the deadly fire, heat and smoke.

fire in makeshift offices loaned by First National City Bank.

Adolpho Cilento Neto, a floor supervisor at the Crefisul Bank Building, recalled that during the fire, he had to hit several fellow workers in the face to subdue their panic and keep them from jumping off the hot roof.

The light rain that had slowed the morning traffic also had impeded the effort to rush fire fighting equipment to the scene. A police investigation report said the flames "spread rapidly upward and to the sides from one floor to another, shattering glass and burning curtains with such violence and speed that in 30 minutes they had reached the top floor of the building."

Another police report alleged that the wiring that touched off the conflagration was of substandard quality, and that proper safety fuses needed to prevent electrical overheating were not being used.

A Crefisul official said that before the disaster, the bank had planned to install a fire escape in the structure. They never did.

And, police said, fire hydrants on each floor of the building were without water during the blaze because the valves on two rooftop tanks were unexplainedly closed.

Criticism also centered on São Paulo's antiquated building code.

A week after the fire, Mayor Miguel Colasuonno issued an emergency decree imposing new fire safety standards on construction. The decree required new buildings more than 115 feet high to contain roof platforms designed to protect building occupants from heat and fire and to support the weight of helicopters.

It also required new buildings to have automatic sprinkler systems, fireproof stairways and elevator shafts, and a fireproof room on each floor.

The survivors would find little solace in Mayor Colasuonno's disclosure that on the day of the fire, existing regulations in the old building code had gone unenforced for years.

# THE NIGHT THE EARTH DANCED

**T**his aerial photo shows the village of San Martin Jil-otepeque almost in total ruins. Nearly 3,000 people lost their lives there.

**W**orkers begin the long task of clearing the streets in Guatemala City several days after the earthquake. This view shows the destruction suffered in one of the city's poorer sections.

**T**his destroyed bridge at Aguas Calientes outside Guatemala City testifies to the tremendous force of the predawn earthquake. Landslide and felled bridges hampered rescue efforts to the hard-hit countryside.

Juan Rumpich Chay, his wife and children were sound asleep in their tiny adobe home in the town of Chimaltenango, Guatemala, in the early morning hours of Wednesday, February 4, 1976.

At about 3 A.M., Juan and his family awoke in terror. The whole world seemed to be shaking. Their ears filled with the din of falling walls and people screaming.

"I prayed in the dark, eyes wide open, that God would stop this awful punishment," Juan recalled later.

In that moment, thousands upon thousands died in what would be one of the most devastating earthquakes in this century. In nature's most awesome of demonstrations, death and destruction were dealt to much of Guatemala, and the tremors would be felt in Mexico, Honduras and El Salvador.

In the initial quake and a series of aftershocks, upwards of 22,000 people perished, another 75,000 were injured and one-sixth of the nation's six million people were left homeless.

And in Chimaltenango, a town of 21,000, Juan Rumpich Chay's nightmare was just beginning.

"I ran to the door and it was blocked," Juan said. "The earth shook violently for a full minute before I could open the door, using all the strength of my body. My father was crying for help. I ran to his room, crawling and climbing over the debris that had been my home."

Juan found his father partially buried under mud bricks and roof tiles, but still alive. "It took me half an hour to free him and one of his legs was broken."

Then Juan rushed to the rubble of what had been his mother's room. With the help of a neighbor, Juan found his mother under a three-foot pile of debris. She was dead, her body bent double by the terrible weight, her head bowed between her knees as if in prayer. They carried the body outside to a courtyard and placed it on the damp ground.

The sun rose over Guatemala shortly after 6 A.M., permitting the first aircraft to fly over the rugged countryside. It was evident that much of Guatemala lay in ruins.

Chimaltenango counted 3,000 dead. Elsewhere, whole villages were leveled, their rooftops resting on flattened buildings. Houses crumbled all across the countryside, at Indian villages with ancient names such as Tecpán, Patzicía, Putzal, Zupangon Joyabaj, San Martin Jilotepeque and others.

Guatemala City, the capital, was not as badly hit, although damage and casualties were high in the crowded working class neighborhoods, where houses fell, water lines were broken and electricity was cut off for several days.

The big aftershocks of the quake sent thousands of people into the streets and parks, wailing in fear.

"¿Porqué, Dios mio? ¿Porqué, Dios mio?" one man screamed. "Why, my God? Why, my God?"

In Chimaltenango, Juan gathered his family in the courtyard. He, his wife, Juana, their four children, a sister and her child held one another in a tight group in the dark, dusty hours until dawn.

"We stayed there because the earth still shook strongly," he said. "My throat was bitter. We expected another earthquake. We tried to talk to God because we knew he was punishing us, not just us but everyone. Because everything comes from God, the good and the bad."

After the sun rose, Juan hitched a chair to his back, loaded his injured father into it, and walked to a nearby hospital. Others were arriving with similar burdens.

Later that afternoon, Juan and his brother Jose fashioned a crude coffin from the splintered wood of Juan's house and they buried their 55-year-old mother in the town cemetery, alone, without a priest. By nightfall, hundreds of others had been buried in a common grave.

Juan and his family went to bed that night with empty stomachs, trying to sleep on the ground beside the ruins of their home.

"We hadn't eaten because we weren't hungry," he said. "I lay next to my wife and some of the children and asked God not to touch our land again."

Cathleen Chandler, 20-year-old daughter of *Los Angeles Times* publisher Otis Chandler, was staying with a Guatemalan family in Antigua when the quake struck.

"I woke up completely stricken by the feeling that not just the bed, or the room, but that the whole city was shaking. You could feel the intensity of it in your bones.

"I was so frozen with fear I could not get out of bed for five or ten seconds. . . . It was completely dark. I remember running and groping for the door."

Miss Chandler, one of 40 American students in Antigua for a language institute, said a wall of the house had collapsed, injuring two of the sons of her host family. One later died of his injuries.

Antigua, a colonial city famed for its magnificent buildings and churches left by the Spanish conquerors, was severely damaged. Crumpled church belfries lay in heaps.

Shirley Joseph of Lawrence, Kansas, a tourist, was staying in a ninth-floor room of the Camino Real Hotel in Guatemala City when the quake hit.

"Everything started falling in the bathroom. I tried to get out when my husband shouted it was an earthquake. We just grabbed each other. Then we started down the stairs. The ground was moving under our feet."

Within hours after the quake, a radio broadcast in Guatemala City was announcing: "The morgue is full. Please don't bring any more bodies to the morgue."

Many people wandered in a daze through the debris-choked city streets. Rescue efforts at first were hampered by rubble, scattered small fires and at least 15 immediate aftershocks that brought down already weakened walls. A dormant volcano near the city was spouting smoke when dawn broke.

Because communications across the country had been so badly disrupted by the earthquake, it would be several days before the full extent of the catastrophe was known.

Getting food, medicine, water and manpower to the hardest hit regions outside of Guatemala City was made nearly impossible by landslides and collapsed bridges.

Along a 50-mile strip north of the capital, four towns lay in little more than dust. From the air, Indian women wearing bright orange and purple blouses could be seen digging through the rubble, searching for survivors and belongings.

From a high altitude over Patzicía,

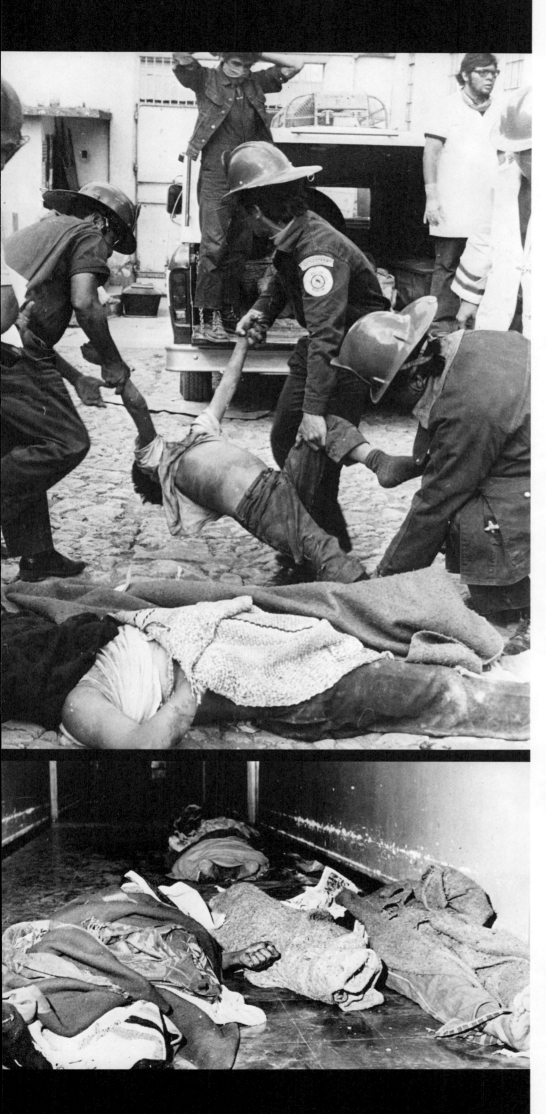

which had a population of 11,000, the rooftops appeared to be intact. But as the pilot dropped lower, it could be seen that the walls of the buildings had collapsed and most of the roofs were flat on the ground.

Disease, rain and chilly weather—and the continuing aftershocks—added to the miseries of the homeless survivors. Doctors pleaded for serum to fight an outbreak of typhoid and other diseases spread by contaminated water.

And some residents began arming themselves against another problem—looting. Guatemalan police said that at least two looters were shot and killed by homeowners during the weekend.

In the capital, lumber for coffins ran out and officials appealed for fast burials, fearing that an accumulation of bodies would bring outbreaks of disease. Corpses in the streets were draped with dusty sheets of plastic. Others were stacked in the General Hospital patio, in offices and in the hospital chapel.

General Fernando Lucas, the national defense minister, threatened to withhold food supplies from the little town of San Martin Jilotepeque because, he said, survivors there refused to continue burying the dead unless they were paid for their labors.

The few travelers who arrived from the interior regions brought reports of horrible destruction there. Ruins blocked the highways and country roads, and landslides had left huge scars on the green hillsides. Clouds of dust continued to billow into the air from new landslides triggered by aftershocks. The towns of Zumpango and Juan Comalapa, about 25 miles west of the capital, were in total ruins with many dead and injured.

"It was a pathetic scene," said Alphonso Bravo, an employee of the newspaper *Prensa Libre*. "The dead were just being laid in this huge hole. There were many people injured, but they had no medical attention. They were just suffering."

In San Lucas village, just 10 miles from Guatemala City, 100 women lined up for meat from a cow killed in the quake. They had to fight off hungry dogs to get a scrap

**R**escue workers lift the lifeless body of a small boy into a vehicle for transportation to the overcrowded morgue in the small village of San Luis Zacatepec.

**I**n Guatemala City, the dead were laid in hospital corridors when the morgues filled up. At least 2,000 people died in the capital city.

**S**ome of the dead from the village of Rio de Ververena are buried in a mass grave—a way thousands of others were buried all over Guate-

from the carcass. One woman, who arrived too late, sobbed: "Everything is closed and I don't even have a piece of bread for my children."

Even as tremors continued to wrack the country in the aftermath of the worst earthquake to hit Central America, a massive worldwide relief effort was underway.

Tons of food and medical supplies began pouring in from the United States, Mexico and several other Latin American countries via airlift. The supplies included a 100-bed field hospital airlifted from Ft. Sill, Oklahoma. Other aid came from Canada, and as far away as Belgium and Israel.

In fact, emergency supplies arrived from other countries in such great quantities that Guatemalan officials had to temporarily suspend incoming relief flights because of airport jams.

The relief effort encountered other special problems along the way. Four United States helicopters were delayed from taking off because Mexico at first refused to let them fly over its territory. A law in Mexico forbids overflights by foreign military planes in peacetime. President Luis Echeverria temporarily lifted the ban.

And two planeloads of British aid were refused by the Guatemalan government "for reasons of national dignity." Guatemala and Britain were feuding over Belize, an 8,000-square-mile British colony adjoining Guatemala, which claimed it.

But Guatemala President Kjell Eugenio Laugerud would observe later: "As usual, it is the people with the least means who suffer the most in these tragedies."

The worst damage in Guatemala City was in the rundown central area where the poor usually buy their food day by day. Many markets and shops were destroyed and food prices skyrocketed in the few stores that opened for business. The prices of sugar and frijole beans doubled; bread which sold for six cents a roll was selling for twenty-five cents in stores that had any.

Poor residents, who normally have no running water, sometimes fought each other for a cupful at the few public taps that still trickled.

And for Juan Rumpich Chay, in what was left of his village, life went on. He built a sleeping shelter out of sheet metal, matting, burlap sacks and topped it with a cornstalk roof. "I will never again build another house of adobe brick," he said.

And as another tremor shook the ground, Juan and his family again clung to one another in the yard, accepting the wrath of God and wondering when it would all end.

**W**ithin hours after the quake struck, relief supplies began to pour into Guatemala from all over the world. Here, badly needed medicines and supplies are unloaded from a U.S. Air Force C-5A transport at Guatemala City Airport.

**E**mergency food supplies reached these Indian children in the village of Tecpan three days after the earthquake—and it made the difference between life and death.

# LAST VACATION IN SPAIN

**T**he twisted remains of the propane truck that brought death and destruction to a vacationers' campsite on the Mediterranean. *Inset:* Charred debris testifies to the force of the explosion.

FRANCE

ANDORRA

SPAIN

Ebro River

Barcelona

Mediterranean Sea

Tarragona

0        50        100 Miles

The section of coastline south of Barcelona, Spain, is a scenic one, framed on the west by the coastal highway and on the east by the sparkling blue waters of the Mediterranean. One would expect that the campsite along the water's edge near Tarragona, 50 miles south of Barcelona, would be crowded with hundreds of vacationers and campers on a summer's day.

It was particularly congested around the noon hour on July 11, 1978, when many—including entire families—were preparing lunch or settling down for a short siesta.

A freakish accident, however, would shortly turn the area into a flaming nightmare for some, a last vacation for still many others.

Coming around a bend in the highway, a tank truck carrying more than 1,500 cubic feet of liquid industrial gas—propylene—overturned, exploded and tumbled into the campsite, engulfing hundreds of campers in the conflagration.

Flames spewed in all directions, and the force of the blast blew some campers into the sea 150 yards away. Scores of people were incinerated within seconds; many others would linger on with burns so severe that death was inevitable.

Officials said more than 800 campers were at the site four miles from San Carlos de la Rapita, just south of Tarragona. Most of the vacationers were French, West German, British, Dutch and Belgian.

One 28-year-old German woman said, "I felt a heat wave on my back and instinctively plunged into the water. I swam away from the beach towing my 8-year-old daughter who can't swim."

Despite her efforts, however, the woman suffered slight burns and her daughter was

One of the survivors of the Tarragona camp explosion wanders aimlessly through the desolation of the once-attractive campsite.

severely injured. Both were flown to Heidelberg, Germany, and taken to a special burn clinic.

Flaming gas from the truck seemed to set off a chain reaction of exploding cooking gas bottles and automobile gasoline tanks. The blast demolished about 100 camping trailers and destroyed a dozen homes near the campsite.

According to witnesses, the truck had been traveling about 40 miles an hour down the highway when the driver, who was killed in the accident, apparently lost control of the vehicle.

"It has all been horrible," said a municipal policeman who was at the camp when the blast occurred. "All of a sudden there was a terrific explosion and flames engulfed us. Cries came from everywhere in the camp. People could be seen running in all directions to safety. Some were ablaze. And we were helpless to do anything."

Many of the injured, some with burns over 75 per cent of their bodies, were taken to hospitals in Valencia, Tarragona, Castellon de la Plana and Barcelona. The very severely injured were given little hope for survival. Many of the dead were burned so badly that their identities could not be confirmed until weeks later.

Cisternas Reunidas, a Madrid transportation company, took responsibility for the tragedy and ordered an immediate investigation. The company said the 38-ton truck was built in 1974 and had undergone frequent inspections. Later investigation indicated that the truck may have had a tire blowout on the curve.

But for the vacationers who perished in the flames or who died later of their injuries, the cause was of far lesser significance than the effect.

Spanish Civil Guardsmen sift through the wreckage at Tarragona in the search for victims. The blast hurled some victims into the nearby sea.

193

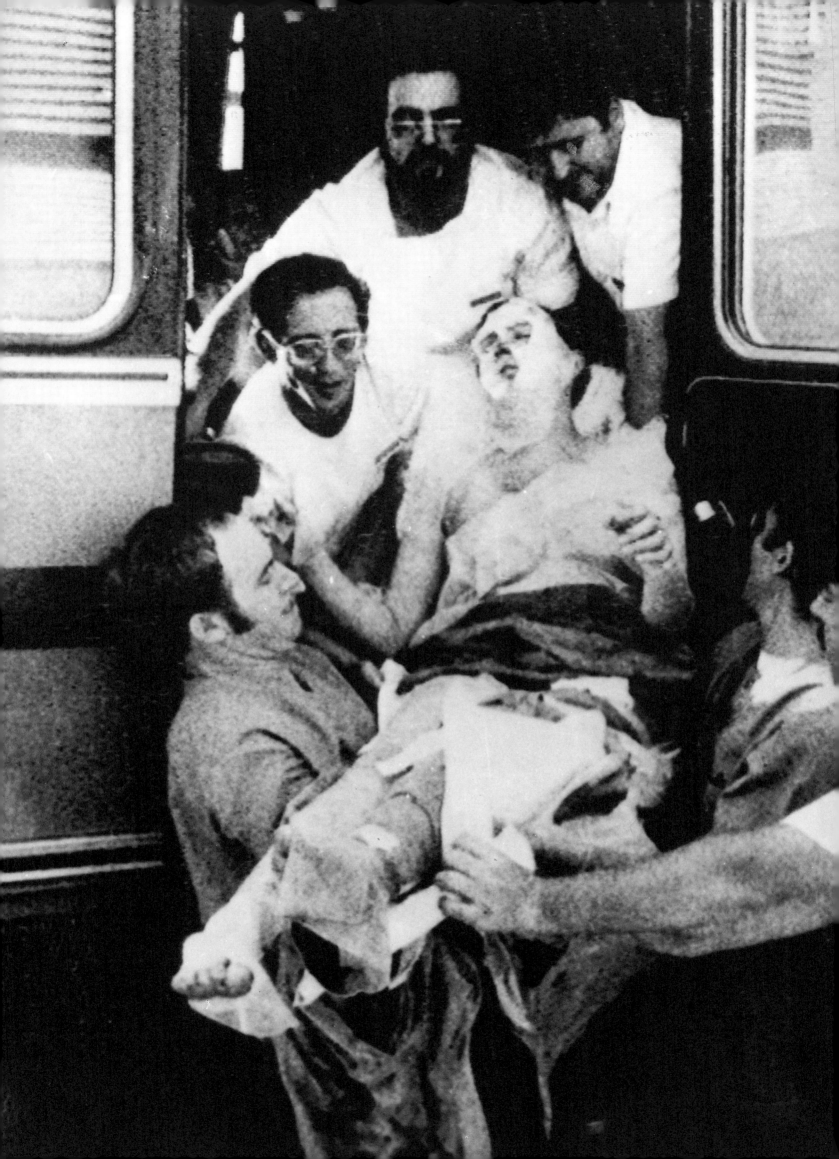

**O**ne of the lucky survivors—despite his severe burns—is shown being transferred to a hospital at Valencia, Spain.

**T**he lifeless bodies of many of the victims lie in coffins as attempts are made to identify the bodies, some of which were burned beyond recognition.

# DAY OF THE VOLCANO

**M**ount St. Helens continues to belch smoke little more than two weeks after an eruption blew off 1,400 feet of its northern flank. *Inset:* A view inside the fiery caldera of Mount St. Helens.

Sunday, May 18, 1980, dawned clear and sunny in Vancouver, in southwest Washington state. Just 40 miles away loomed Mount St. Helens, a picturesque snowcapped peak that makes up part of the beautiful Cascade Range, a string of mountains that comprise part of the "ring of fire" girdling the Pacific Ocean from South America through the Aleutian Islands to Japan.

For two months, geologists had been keeping a wary eye on the mountain because of seismic activity recorded earlier.

But the mountain would wait until this bright Sunday to release its pent-up fury.

At 8:32 A.M., two quick earthquakes shook the 9,677-foot peak and broke off a blister of ice and rock that had been bulging from its north slope. Suddenly, a wall of rock where the bulge had been blew out with a force of 10 million tons of TNT.

The eruption ripped about 1,200 feet off the top of the mountain, blew hot ash 13 miles into the sky, and dusted cities and farms in four states. About 150 square miles of scenic countryside surrounding Mount St. Helens turned into a deathscape.

The unstoppable flow of ash, rock slides and mudflows left 57 people dead, or missing and presumed dead.

The belching hot gas and ash blotted out the sun for more than 450 miles, and the blast spawned a mile-wide wall of mud that oozed down the north fork of the Toutle River, snapping steel bridges like toothpicks and sweeping cars and houses in its path.

In Walla Walla, 160 miles to the east, drifting ash made the sky so dark that automatic streetlights went on, and by evening, more than a foot of ash had accumulated at Camp Baker, 15 miles west of the volcano. Even as far east as Montana, some roads were closed because of near-zero visibility caused by falling ash.

Near the mountain, the bodies of two people were found at a logging camp.

"These people were fried by the heat," said Air Force Captain Robert Wead. "Trees and all the vegetation were laid out flat—singed, burned, steaming, sizzling—a terrible-looking thing."

The landscape surrounding Mount St. Helens did, indeed, look hellish. Three billion board feet of timber—enough to build 200,000 three-bedroom homes—were blown over.

About 2,000 people were evacuated from the town of Toutle and nearby low-lying regions 30 miles northwest of the mountain. Most people living closer to the volcano site had left weeks earlier. But not crusty Harry Truman, who ran Mount St. Helens Lodge on Spirit Lake at the base of the thundering mountain. The 84-year-old Truman, no relation to the former President, refused to leave his place just seven miles north of the summit. By evening, more than 30 feet of mud and debris had covered the 40-acre resort, and nothing ever was seen of Harry Truman again. He has since become a legend to the local people.

Others were not so unfortunate.

"It's a miracle I'm still alive," said Sue Ruff. She and a friend escaped death under a canopy of freakishly arranged falling trees, while others in their camping party were crushed beneath crashing timber.

Today, Mount St. Helens, while still thundering and belching gases every now and then, has already begun its rebirth. Flowers and trees have begun sprouting on the desolate landscape and animal life has returned to the area.

Even in Spirit Lake, scientists have found microorganisms believed to be like those present when life began on this planet.

**M**ount St. Helens, 45 miles northeast of Portland, Washington, remains active to this day. This view shows the volcano spewing smoke and ash during a minor eruption.

The initial eruption poured ash for miles around. Ash and forest debris covered these vehicles as rescue efforts were mounted for the dead and missing.

**A** tragic volcano victim was found here in his car, buried under tons of debris from Mount St. Helens.

**H**omes and businesses at Toutle, Washington, about 20 miles from the base of the angry mountain, suffered heavy damage from the flooded Toutle River. In this photo, cleanup operations have begun.

**O**tto Sieber, a photographer from Seattle, is assisted by Army medics after his rescue by helicopter from near the volcano.

**T**all, denuded fir trees lay toppled like toothpicks from the force of the eruption. The volcano destroyed 100,000 acres of timber.

**E**ruptions from Mount St. Helens triggered flash floods and mudslides that caused heavy damage to houses like this one along the Toutle River.

**A**lice Merkel of Yale, Washington, carries her son, Eddie, into a grange hall where temporary housing was established. Local residents were evacuated in the wake of eruptions on Mount St. Helens.

# DANCE OF DEATH

**R**escue workers probe the wreckage in the lobby of the Hyatt Regency Hotel, the scene of a tea dance shortly before the skywalks fell.

A solitary guest walks by the wreckage—scene of death and destruction two nights before. Two overhead walkways had plunged to the floor, killing and maiming hundreds of guests.

The Steve Miller Band was playing Duke Ellington's "Satin Doll," and the contestants in the Friday-night dance contest were already on the floor.

This weekly "tea dance," featuring the music of the big band era, already had become a fixture at Kansas City's new Hyatt Regency Hotel, which had opened its doors a year earlier, in 1980.

The stunning 40-story structure had been built at a cost of $50 million and contained 733 suites and rooms. But the showcase of the hotel was its spectacular five-story lobby, almost the size of a football field. And two overhead walkways, one of them spanning about 75 yards, had been billed as one of the most elegant features of the hotel when it opened. They were called "sky bridges," and they connected tower and convention facilities with the main part of the 15,000-square-foot lobby that architects had patterned after the 113-year-old Galleria of Milan, Italy.

The atrium lobby formed a canopied skylight that many visitors said was the most beautiful in Kansas City.

The hotel itself, owned by a subsidiary of Hallmark Cards, Inc., and managed by the Hyatt Hotels Corporation, is located on 3.2 acres about two miles south of downtown Kansas City.

But of those who turned out that night of July 17, 1981, for a nostalgic replay of ballroom dancing—or stopped by for any one of a dozen reasons—scores would leave by ambulance.

And 114 would die.

Shortly after 7 P.M., a loud boom was heard and the fourth-floor walkway split in two places near the center and spilled down on a second-floor sky bridge, which also collapsed. Hundreds of patrons seated, dancing and mingling in the lobby below disappeared from view in the blast of wind and shattering glass.

Also crushed between the two spans were dozens of people who had been leaning over the glass rail watching the dancers below. Under the steel, concrete and glass debris—six feet of it in places—were the dead and injured. Arms, legs and torsos could be seen protruding from the wreckage.

"I couldn't believe it; it just started crashing, caving in," said Dorothy Johnson, a nurse who was having dinner overlooking the lobby. "We just sat there and watched it cave in."

Randy Dunford, another patron whose wife was just about to step onto a crosswalk when it fell, described the scene: "There was a rumbling sound, exactly like a rolling clap of thunder outside, and everything got real quiet for a moment, then there was mass confusion."

**T**he mangled remains of some of the 114 victims lie under the wreckage of the skywalks. Rescue workers had a grim and arduous duty to perform in locating and identifying those who lost their lives.

Kansas City Royals pitcher Rich Gale, who was working as a bartender that night—during the major league baseball strike—said it "took two, three or four seconds, maybe. Then there was a loud roar, then rushing, hissing . . . human sounds started immediately."

Hundreds of rescue workers began arriving on the scene within minutes. As the first of the bodies were pulled from the tangle of twisted metal and shattered glass, officials designated a ground-floor exhibition area as a temporary morgue. There a priest administered last rites.

One veteran fireman, among the first to arrive at the scene, said, "It was like walking into the middle of a horror movie with the sound turned off. There was no screaming. There was no panic. There was hardly a sound. It seemed unnatural."

Rescue operations continued into the next day, and some discoveries were happy ones: 10 injured people were found, and searchers cheered when they lifted survivors from the rubble. But most were grim. The last 31 bodies were found buried together under a heavy concrete slab.

One rescue worker told how he pulled a girl out of the rubble and she cried, "My sister's back there." Rescue workers went back and found her dead.

One firefighter told of rescuers hearing the moans of a trapped 11-year-old boy about five hours after the collapse. He said he lay on his stomach for more than an hour talking to the youngster over the noise of jackhammers and blowtorches. They finally rescued the boy, along with his injured parents, also buried under the rubble.

And from time to time, as workers probed the wreckage for other victims, helium-filled balloons, remnants of the party that was no more, drifted aloft.

Following a seven-month investigation, the National Bureau of Standards concluded that a critical design change in the skywalk support structure caused the collapse, not faulty workmanship or materials.

Millions of out-of-court settlements have been made, but no amount of money will allay the memories of those who were injured or had friends or family members perish in the accident.

Said one witness who was uninjured but lost friends in the tragedy, "I get dressed and all ready to go somewhere. And then I'll get tired, or just find some reason not to go. Sometimes I'll stay home and sit in the dark."

Emergency medical treatment is given to one of the injured as he awaits extraction from under the collapsed concrete and steel.

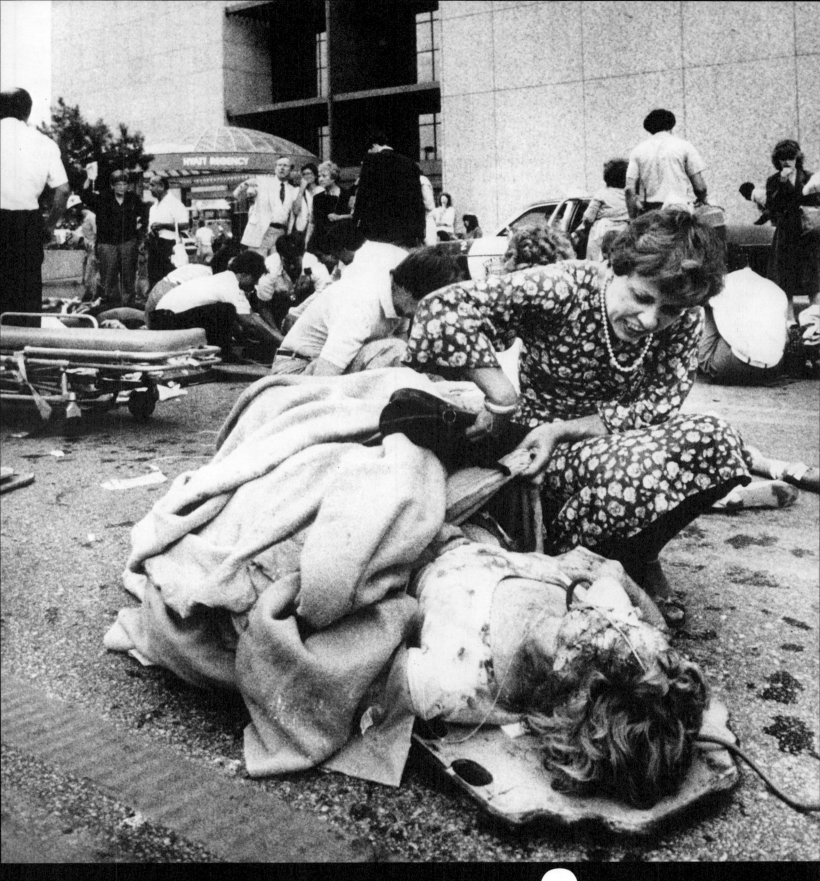

**O**ne woman gives comfort to another as she lies in the street outside the hotel before being taken to a hospital by ambulance.

# APPENDIX:

## MAJOR DISASTERS SINCE 1900

Following is a list of memorable disasters of the 20th century. It encompasses the "natural" disasters such as earthquakes, volcanic eruptions, epidemics and storms and the "technological" catastrophes of rail and airplane crashes, shipwrecks, mine accidents, fires and explosions. Attempts to limit the list to disasters above a certain death toll were abandoned not only because of insufficient information in many cases, but also because it was too arbitrary. A number of calamities that resulted in few fatalities have been cited because of their significance and/or their freshness in our memories. It should be noted that some governments are reluctant to issue reports of disasters, possibly due to national sensitivities, expecially when the cause is technical failure. The list is, however, as comprehensive as available data and space permits. It is worldwide in scope.

### 1900

| | |
|---|---|
| China and India | Bubonic plague killed 3 (?) million between 1898 and 1908. |
| Hoboken, N.J. | Pier fire, over 300 dead, damage $4.6 million; June 30. |
| Galveston, Tex. | Hurricane and high tides wreck city, 6000 (?) dead; Aug. 27-Sept. 15. |

### 1902

| | |
|---|---|
| Martinique, West Indies | Volcanic eruption of Mt. Pelée destroys city of Pierre, over 30,000 dead; May 8. |
| Birmingham, Ala. | Church fire, 115 dead; Sept. 20. |

### 1903

| | |
|---|---|
| Heppner, Ore. | Flood destroys town, over 250 dead; May. |
| Chicago, Ill. | Iroquois Theater fire, about 600 dead; Dec. 30. |

### 1904

| | |
|---|---|
| Cheswick, Pa. | Coal mine explosion, 179 dead; Jan. 25. |
| New York, N.Y. | Steamer *General Slocum* burns in East River, over 1,000 dead; June 15. |
| Rockall Reef, Scotland | Shipwreck of *Norge*, about 600 dead; June 28. |

### 1905

| | |
|---|---|
| Courrières, France | Mine explosion, 1,060 dead; Mar. 10. |

### 1906

| | |
|---|---|
| San Francisco, Calif. | Earthquake followed by fire destroys most of city, 700 (?) dead, 250,000 homeless and $524 million in property damage; Apr. 18 |
| Valparaiso and Santiago, Chile | Earthquake causes widespread damage, 5,000 dead, estimated property loss $100 million; April 18. |
| Off Cape Palos, Italy | Italian ship *Sirio* wrecked, 350 dead; Aug. 4 |
| Hong Kong | Tropical typhoon takes over 50,000 lives; Sept. 19. |
| Washington, D.C. | Train wreck, 53 dead; Dec. 20. |

### 1907

| | |
|---|---|
| India | Bubonic plague kills 1.3 million. |
| Stuart, W. Va. | Coal mine explosion, 84 dead; Jan. 29. |
| Off Long Island | Steamer *Larchmont* sinks, 131 lost; Feb. 12. |
| Monongah, W. Va. | Coal mine explosion, 362 dead; Dec. 6. |
| Jacobs Creek, Pa. | Coal mine explosion, 239 dead; Dec. 19. |

### 1908

| | |
|---|---|
| Boyertown, Pa. | Fire in Rhoads Opera House cinema kills over 100; Jan. 13. |

212

| | |
|---|---|
| Collinwood, Ohio | School fire, 161 dead; Mar. 4. |
| Chelsea, Mass. | Fire destroys city, $17 million damage; Apr. 12. |
| Southern Italy and Sicily | Earthquake takes 100,000 (?) lives and leaves one million homeless; Dec. 28. |

### 1909

| | |
|---|---|
| Acapulco, Mex. | Flores Theater fire, 250 (?) dead; Feb. 15. |
| Louisiana and Mississippi | Tropical storm kills 350; Sept. 19–21. |
| Cherry, Ill. | Coal mine fire, 259 dead; Nov. 13. |

### 1909–18

| | |
|---|---|
| China and India | Bubonic plague fatal for 1.5 million (?). |

### 1910

| | |
|---|---|
| Primero, Calif. | Coal mine explosion, 75 dead; Jan. 31. |
| Wellington, Wash. | Avalanche sweeps two trains into canyon, 96 dead; Mar. 1. |
| Palos, Ala. | Coal mine explosion, 90 dead; May 5. |
| Delague, Colo. | Coal mine explosion, 79 dead; Nov. 8. |
| Manchuria | Pneumonic plague kills 60,000 (?); 1910–1911. |

### 1911

| | |
|---|---|
| China | Flood of Yangtze River, 100,000 (?) dead. |
| New York, N.Y. | Fire in Triangle Shirtwaist Factory kills 147; Mar. 25. |
| Littleton, Ala. | Coal mine explosion, 128 dead; Apr. 8. |
| Briceville, Tenn. | Coal mine explosion, 84 dead; Dec. 9. |

### 1912

| | |
|---|---|
| Off Spain | Steamer *Principe de Asturias* wrecked, 500 drowned; Mar. 5. |
| McCurtain, Okla. | Coal mine explosion, 73 dead; Mar. 20. |
| Jed, W. Va. | Coal mine explosion, 83 dead; Mar. 26. |
| North Atlantic | Liner *Titanic* strikes iceberg and sinks on maiden voyage, 1,500 (?) dead; Apr. 15. |
| Off Japan | Japanese *Kichermaru* sinks, 1,000 lost; Sept. 28. |

### 1913

| | |
|---|---|
| Omaha, Neb. | Tornado kills 100; Mar. 23. |
| Eastern United States | Floods in 7 states, 500 (?) lives lost, damages of $515 million; Mar. 25–27. |
| Finleyville, Pa. | Coal mine explosion, 96 dead; Apr. 23. |
| Dawson, N. Mex. | Coal mine explosion, 263 died; Oct. 22. |

### 1914

| | |
|---|---|
| Eccles, W. Va. | Coal mine explosion, 183 dead; Apr. 28. |
| St. Lawrence R., Canada | Canadian Pacific liner *Empress of Ireland* collides with collier and sinks, 1,024 dead; May 29. |
| Salem, Mass. | Fire destroys 1,700 buildings, damages $14 million; June 25–26. |

### 1915

| | |
|---|---|
| Central Italy | Earthquake, 30,000 (?) dead; Jan. 13. |
| Layland, W. Va. | Coal mine explosion, 112 dead; Mar. 2. |
| Off Ireland | Liner *Lusitania* sunk by German submarine, 1,198 dead; May 7 |
| Gretna, Scotland | Three-train collision, 227 dead; May 22. |
| Chicago River, Ill. | Excursion boat *Eastland* capsizes in port, 812 dead; July 24. |
| Serbia | Typhus epidemic claims 150,000. |
| Texas and Louisiana | Hurricane, 275 (?) dead; Aug. 5–25. |
| United States Gulf Coast | Hurricane, over 250 dead; Sept. 22-Oct. 1. |

### 1916

| | |
|---|---|
| Mediterranean Sea | French cruiser *Provence* sinks, 3,100 (?) dead; Feb. 26. |
| Jersey City, N.J. | German sabotage (explosion and fire) on Black Tom Island kills 4, damage $14 million; July 30. |
| Off China | *Hsin Yu* sinks, 1,000 (?) dead; Aug. 29. |

### 1917

| | |
|---|---|
| Chester, Pa. | Explosion in munitions plant kills 125; Apr. 10. |
| Halifax Harbor, Canada | Explosion of munitions aboard S.S. *Mont Blanc* after collision destroys city, 1,400 dead; Dec. 6. |
| Modane, France | Troop train derailment, 550 (?) dead; Dec. 12. |

### 1917–19

| | |
|---|---|
| Worldwide | Influenza pandemic kills 20–30 million. |

### 1917–21

| | |
|---|---|
| Russia | Typhus epidemic kills 2.5-3 million. |

### 1918

| | |
|---|---|
| Barbados, West Indies | U.S.S. *Cyclops* lost at sea; 280 dead; Mar. 4 |
| Nashville, Tenn. | Head-on train collision, 100 (?) dead; July 9. |
| Tokyo Bay, Japan | Japanese battleship *Kawachi* explodes, 500 (?) dead; July 12. |
| Puerto Rico | Earthquake and tidal wave, 116 dead and severe damage; Oct. 11. |

| | |
|---|---|
| Minnesota and Wisconsin | Forest fire kills about 1,000, damages $100 million; Oct. 13–15. |
| Brooklyn, N.Y. | Subway train derailment, 92 dead. |

**1919**

| | |
|---|---|
| Strait of Messina | French steamer *Chaonia* wrecked, 460 dead; Jan. 17. |
| San Juan, Puerto Rico | Mayaguez Theater fire, 150 dead; June 20. |
| Florida, Louisiana and Texas | Hurricane kills 287; Sept. 2–15. |

**1920**

| | |
|---|---|
| India | Bubonic plague claims 2 (?) million; 1920's. |
| Kansu, China | Earthquake kills 180,000 (?), ten cities destroyed; Dec. 16. |

**1921**

| | |
|---|---|
| India | Cholera epidemic, 500,000 (?) dead. |
| Off Swatow, China | Steamer *Hong Kong* wrecked on rocks, 1,000 (?) dead; Mar. 18. |
| Hall, England | British dirigible *ZR-2* breaks in two, 62 dead; Aug. 24. |
| Oppau, Germany | Ammonium nitrate explosion kills 600 (?); Sept. 21. |

**1922**

| | |
|---|---|
| Smyrna, Asia Minor | Fire destroys most of city, hundreds dead, damage $100 million; Sept. 13. |

**1923**

| | |
|---|---|
| Dawson, N. Mex. | Coal mine explosion, 120 dead; Feb. 8. |
| Tokyo and Yokohama, Japan | Earthquake followed by fire destroys most of both cities, 200,000 (?) dead; Sept 1. |
| Berkeley, Calif. | Fire destroys 600 buildings, $12.5 million damage; Sept. 17. |
| Mediterranean Sea or Sahara Desert | French dirigible *Dixmude* disappears, 50 lost; Dec. 21. |

**1924**

| | |
|---|---|
| India | Cholera epidemic, 300,000 (?) dead. |
| Castle Gate, Utah | Coal mine explosion, 171 dead; Mar. 8. |
| Benwood, W. Va. | Coal mine explosion, 119 dead; Apr. 28. |

**1925**

| | |
|---|---|
| Sullivan, Ind. | Coal mine explosion, 52 dead; Feb. 20. |
| Midwest U.S. | Tornado sweeps through Missouri, Illinois and Indiana, 689 killed; Mar. 18. |

| | |
|---|---|
| Lorain and Sandusky, Ohio | Tornado kills 85, damage $12 million; June 28. |

**1926–30**

| | |
|---|---|
| India | Smallpox epidemic claims 423,000 (?). |

**1926**

| | |
|---|---|
| Florida and Alabama | Hurricane kills 243; Sept. 11–22. |
| Havana, Cuba | Hurricane claims 600 lives, Oct. 20. |

**1927**

| | |
|---|---|
| Everettville, W. Va. | Coal mine explosion, 97 dead; Apr. 30. |
| St. Louis, Mo. | Tornado hits city, 90 dead and damage of $40 million; Sept. 29. |
| Arkansas | Tornado kills 92; May 9. |

**1928**

| | |
|---|---|
| Santa Paula, Calif. | St. Francis dam collapses, 450 dead; Mar. 13. |
| Mather, Pa. | Coal mine explosion, 195 dead; May 19. |
| Southern Florida | Hurricane and overflow of Lake Okeechobee, 1,836 lives lost; Sept. 6–20. |
| Off Virginia capes | British steamer *Vestris* sinks, 110 (?) dead; Nov. 12. |

**1929**

| | |
|---|---|
| Cleveland, Ohio | Hospital fire, 125 suffocations from poisonous fumes; May 15. |
| McAlester, Okla. | Coal mine explosion, 61 dead; Dec. 17. |

**1930**

| | |
|---|---|
| Columbus, Ohio | Fire at Ohio State Penitentiary kills 317 convicts; Apr. 21. |
| Naples, Italy | Earthquake claims 1,883 and injures 10,000 (?); July 23–25. |
| Dominican Republic | Hurricane kills 2,000 (?); Oct. 5. |
| Beauvais, France | British dirigible *R-101* crashes, 47 dead; Oct. 5. |
| Millfield, Ohio | Coal mine explosion, 82 dead; Nov. 5. |

**1931**

| | |
|---|---|
| Off St.-Nazaire, France | French excursion steamer *St. Philibert* capsizes, 450 lost; June 14. |
| Yangtze River, China | Flood claims 140,000 lives, over 2 million homeless; July-Aug. |

**1932**

| | |
|---|---|
| Southern United States | Tornadoes hit five states, at least 362 dead; Mar. 21–22. |
| Kansu, China | Earthquakes claim 70,000 (?); Dec. 26. |

**1933**

| | |
|---|---|
| Sanriku coast, Japan | Earthquake kills more than 2,500; Mar. 3. |

| | | | |
|---|---|---|---|
| Off New Jersey | U.S. dirigible *Akron II* crashes at sea, 73 dead; Apr. 4. | Northeast and Midwest U.S. | Blizzard caused 144 deaths, damages of $6 million; Nov. 11–12. |

**1934**

| | |
|---|---|
| Hakodate, Japan | Fire destroys city, 1,500 dead; Mar. 22. |
| Off New Jersey | Liner *Morro Castle* burns, 134 dead; Sept. 8. |
| Honshu, Japan | Typhoon kills 4,000 (?), damage over $50 million; Sept. 21. |
| Wrexham, Wales | Coal mine explosion, 265 dead; Sept. 22. |

**1935**

| | |
|---|---|
| Uganda | Bubonic plague kills 2,000 (?). |
| India and Pakistan | Earthquake kills over 50,000; May 31. |
| Southern Florida | Hurricane claims 408 lives, damage up to $50 million; Aug. 29-Sept. 10. |
| Haiti | Hurricane kills 2,000; Oct. 22. |

**1936**

| | |
|---|---|
| Southern United States | Tornado series, mostly in Mississippi and Georgia, kills 455, damage $21 million; Apr. 5–6. |

**1937**

| | |
|---|---|
| Antung, Manchuria | Theater fire kills 658; Feb. 13. |
| New London, Tex. | Natural gas explosion in school, 296 dead; Mar. 18. |
| Lakehurst, N.J. | German zeppelin *Hindenburg* explodes, 36 dead; May 6. |

**1938**

| | |
|---|---|
| Bogotá, Colombia | Military stunt plane crashes into grandstand killing 53; July 24. |
| New England and Long Island | Hurricane kills over 600, property damage up to $500 million; Sept. 21. |

**1939**

| | |
|---|---|
| Chile | Earthquake claims 40,000 (?), 700,000 homeless; Jan. 24. |
| Off New Hampshire | U.S. submarine *Squalus* sinks, 26 lost; May 23. |
| In the Irish Sea | British submarine *Thetis* sinks, 99 dead; June 1. |
| Off Indochina | French submarine *Phoenix* sinks, 63 dead; June 15. |
| Tientsin, China | Floods render millions homeless and thousands dead; July-Aug. |
| Langunillas, Venezuela | Fire destroys oil town built over Lake Maracaibo; Nov. 14. |
| Magdeburg, Germany | Train collision, 132 dead; Dec. 22. |
| Anatolia, Turkey | Earthquakes and subsequent floods kill over 30,000; Dec. 27. |

**1940**

| | |
|---|---|
| Osaka, Japan | Train collision, 200 (?) dead; Jan. 29. |

**1941**

| | |
|---|---|
| Off Maine | U.S. submarine *O-9* sinks in test dive, 33 lost; June 16. |

**1942**

| | |
|---|---|
| Honkeiko Colliery, Manchuria | Worst mine disaster in history, 1,549 dead; Apr. 26. |
| Off England | British *Curaçao* rammed and sunk by *Queen Mary;* over 330 dead; Oct. 2. |
| Bengal, India | Cyclone claims 40,000 (?); Oct. 16. |
| Boston, Mass. | Cocoanut Grove nightclub fire, 492 dead, 166 injured; Nov. 28. |

**1943**

| | |
|---|---|
| Philadelphia, Pa. | *Congressional Limited* derails, 80 dead; Sept. 6. |
| Lumberton, N.C. | Train collision, 72 dead; Dec. 16. |

**1944**

| | |
|---|---|
| San Juan, Argentina | Earthquake kills 5,000 (?); Jan. 15. |
| León Province, Spain | Train wreck in tunnel causes over 500 deaths; Jan. 16. |
| Near Salerno, Italy | Train stalls in tunnel, 526 suffocated; Mar. 2. |
| Hartford, Conn. | Circus fire claims 168 lives; July 6. |
| Port Chicago, Calif. | Explosion at ammunition loading pier, 322 dead; July 17. |
| Freckleton, England | U.S. bomber crashes into school, over 70 dead; Aug. 23. |
| Cleveland, Ohio | Liquid gas tank explosion sets fire to 50-block area and kills 130; Oct. 20. |

**1945**

| | |
|---|---|
| Cazadero, Mexico | Train collision, 100 (?) dead; Feb. 1. |
| Bari, Italy | U.S.S. *Liberty* explodes in harbor, 360 dead; Apr. 9. |
| New York, N.Y. | U.S. bomber crashes into Empire State Building, 14 dead; July 28. |

**1946**

| | |
|---|---|
| Near Aracaju, Brazil | Train wreck kills 185; Mar. 20. |
| Alaska, Hawaii and West Coast of United States | Subterranean quake in Alaska causes tidal waves that hit Aleutians, West Coast and Hawaii, 173 dead and $25 million damage in Hawaii; Apr. 1. |
| Atlanta, Ga. | Winecoff Hotel fire, 119 dead; Dec. 7. |

**1947**

| | |
|---|---|
| Off Athens, Greece | Greek ship *Himera* hits mine and sinks, 392 lost; Jan. 19. |
| Centralia, Ill. | Coal mine explosion, 111 dead; Mar. 25. |

| | |
|---|---|
| Southwest United States | Tornadoes in Texas, Oklahoma and Kansas, 167 dead, $10 million damage; Apr. 9. |
| Texas City, Tex. | S.S. *Grandcamp* explodes causing fires and secondary explosions, 512 dead, $51 million damage; Apr. 16. |
| Cadiz, Spain | Dockyard explosion, 147 dead; Aug. 18. |
| Egypt | Cholera epidemic claims over 10,000; Sept.-Dec. |
| Honshu, Japan | Typhoon and floods kill 2,000 (?); Sept. 15–19. |

## 1948

| | |
|---|---|
| Inland Sea, Japan | Freighter *Joo Maru* hits mine and sinks, 250 lost; Jan. 28. |
| Fukui, Japan | Earthquake destroys most of city, over 5,000 dead; July 28. |
| Ludwigshafen, Germany | Explosion and fire at I. G. Farben works, over 200 dead; July 28. |
| Hong Kong | Chemical warehouse explosion and fire kills 135; Sept. 22. |

## 1949

| | |
|---|---|
| Off southern China | Chinese *Taiping* collides with collier and sinks, over 600 dead; Jan. 27. |
| Effingham, Ill. | St. Anthony Hospital fire, 74 dead; Apr. 5. |
| Ecuador | Earthquake razes 50 towns, 6,000 (?) dead, 100,000 homeless; Aug. 5. |
| Toronto, Canada | Cruise ship *Noronic* burns at pier, 120 dead; Sept. 17. |
| Nowy Dwor, Poland | Danzig-Warsaw express train derailed, 200 dead; Oct. 22. |
| Southeast India | Cyclone claims 1,000 (?); Oct. 27. |
| Philippines | Typhoon takes 1,000 (?) lives; Oct. 31. |

## 1950

| | |
|---|---|
| Near Tangua, Brazil | Train plunges into Indius River, 108 dead; Apr. 6. |
| Anhwei Province, China | Flood leaves 10 million homeless and 500 dead; Aug. 14. |
| Assam, India | Earthquake kills 1,500 (?); Aug. 15. |
| Richmond Hill, N.Y. | Commuter train rammed by another, 79 dead; Nov. 22. |

## 1951

| | |
|---|---|
| Comoro Islands | Tornado takes 500 lives; Jan. 4. |
| Woodbridge, N.J. | Commuter train plunges through overpass, 84 dead; Feb. 6. |
| Off Isle of Wight | British submarine *Affray* sinks, 75 lost; Apr. 6. |
| Jacuapa, El Salvador | Earthquake claims over 1,000; May 6. |
| Nova Iguaca, Brazil | Train collides with gasoline truck, 54 dead; June 7. |
| Kansas and Missouri | Flood of Kansas River leaves 200,000 homeless, 41 dead, $1 billion damage; July 2–19. |

| | |
|---|---|
| Manchuria | Flood claims 5,000 lives; Aug. 28. |
| Philippines | Typhoon causes 724 fatalities; Dec. 9–10. |
| Elizabeth, N.J. | Non-scheduled plane plunges into river after takeoff, 56 dead; Dec. 16. |
| West Frankfort, Ill. | Coal mine explosion, 119 dead; Dec. 21. |

## 1952

| | |
|---|---|
| Near Rio de Janeiro | Two-train crash, 119 dead; Mar. 4. |
| Mississippi Valley | Tornadoes kill 229; Mar. 21–22. |
| Moscow, U.S.S.R. | Two Soviet planes collide over Tula Airport, 70 dead; Mar. 27. |
| In the Atlantic | U.S. destroyer-mine sweeper *Hobson* and aircraft carrier *Wasp* collide, *Hobson* sinks, 176 dead; Apr. 26. |
| Rzepin, Poland | Train wreck, 160 dead; July 9. |
| Near Waco, Tex. | Two buses collide, 28 dead; Aug. 4. |
| Harrow-Wealdstone, England | Three-train collision, 112 dead; Oct. 8. |
| Luzon, Philippines | Typhoon leaves 1,000 (?) dead or missing; Oct. 22. |
| Moses Lake, Wash. | U.S. Air Force plane crash, 87 dead; Dec. 20. |

## 1953

| | |
|---|---|
| Off Pusan, S. Korea | Korean liner sinks, 249 dead. |
| Northern Europe | Floods devastate North Sea coastal areas, over 2,000 dead; Jan. 31–Feb. 1. |
| Mexico City, Mexico | Two trolley cars collide, over 60 dead; Feb. 21. |
| Eastern Iran | Earthquake destroys town of Trud, 1,000 dead; Feb. 22. |
| Northwestern Turkey | Earthquake kills 1,200 (?); Mar. 18. |
| Waco, Tex. | Tornado hits downtown Waco, 114 dead, $60 million in damage; May 11. |
| Michigan and Ohio | Tornado series kill 142; June 8. |
| Central Massachusetts | Tornado kills 92, $52 million in damage; June 9. |
| Near Tokyo, Japan | U.S. Air Force plane crash, 129 dead; June 18. |
| Near New Caledonia | French *Monique* vanishes in South Pacific, 120 lost; Aug. 1. |
| Near Waiouru, New Zealand | Wellington-Auckland express plunges into stream, 155 dead; Dec. 24. |

## 1954

| | |
|---|---|
| Off Rhode Island | U.S. aircraft carrier *Bennington* explosion and fire, 103 dead; May 26. |
| Kazvin district, Iran | Flash flood kills 2,000 (?); Aug. 1. |
| Orléansville, Algeria | Earthquake kills 1,600 (?); Sept. 9–12. |
| In Tsugaru Strait, Japan | Japanese ferry *Toya Maru* sinks, 1,172 dead; Sept. 26. |

| | |
|---|---|
| Near Hyderabad, India | Express train plunges from bridge, 137 dead; Sept. 28. |
| Haiti, United States and Canada | Hurricane Hazel kills 410 in Haiti, 99 die in U.S. and 85 in Canada; Oct. 5–18. |

## 1955

| | |
|---|---|
| Yokohama, Japan | Fire in home for aged kills 100 (?); Feb. 16–17. |
| Near Guadalajara, Mexico | Train plunges into canyon, 300 (?) dead; Apr. 3. |
| United States eastern seaboard | Hurricane Diane ravages coast, 184 lives lost, over $500 million damage; Aug. 7–21. |
| Mexico and West Indies | Hurricane takes over 750 lives; Sept. 22–28. |
| Pakistan and India | Floods take 1,700 lives and $63 million in crops lost; Oct. 4. |

## 1956

| | |
|---|---|
| Northern Afghanistan | Earthquakes cause 2,000 deaths; June 10–17. |
| In the Atlantic | Venezuelan airliner crashes south of New York, 74 dead; June 20. |
| Grand Canyon, Arizona | Midair collision of TWA and United airliners, 128 dead; June 30. |
| Off Nantucket, Mass. | Italian *Andrea Doria* and Swedish *Stockholm* collide in fog, sinking the *Andrea Doria*, 50 dead or missing; July 25. |
| Chekiang, China | Typhoon and subsequent flood claim 2,000 lives; Aug. 1. |
| Cali, Colombia | Explosion of seven truckloads of dynamite, 1,200 dead, damage $40 million; Aug. 7. |
| Marcinelle, Belgium | Coal mine fire, 263 dead; Aug. 8. |
| Near Secunderbad, India | Two trains plunge into river as bridge collapses, 121 dead; Sept. 21. |
| Marudaiyar, India | Express train derails, 143 dead; Nov. 23. |

## 1957

| | |
|---|---|
| Warrenton, Mo. | Fire in home for aged, 72 dead; Feb. 17. |
| Near Fayetteville, N.C. | Two trucks collide, 21 dead; June 6. |
| Texas, Louisiana and Mississippi | Hurricane Audrey takes 390 lives and causes damage of $50-500 million; June 25–28. |
| Caspian coast, Iran | Earthquake kills over 1,500; July 2. |
| In the Caspian Sea | U.S.S.R. *Eshghabad* runs aground in storm, 270 dead; Ju'y 14. |
| Quebec, Canada | Airliner crash, 79 dead; Aug. 11. |
| Near Kendai, Jamaica | Train plunges into ravine, 175 dead; Sept. 1. |
| Near Montgomery, West Pakistan | Express train crashes into standing train, 250 dead; Sept. 29. |

| | |
|---|---|
| Outer Mongolia | Earthquake fatal for 1,200 (?); Dec. 2. |
| Near London, Eng. | Two-train collision kills 92; Dec. 4. |
| Western Iran | Earthquakes take 1,392 lives; Dec. 13, 15–17. |

## 1958

| | |
|---|---|
| Near Asanoi, India | Coal mine explosion, over 180 dead; Feb. 19. |
| Near Istanbul | Turkish ferry *Uskudar* sinks, 238 dead; Mar. 1. |
| Near Rio de Janeiro | Two-train collision, 128 dead; May 8. |
| In the Atlantic, west of Ireland | KLM airliner crashes, 99 dead; Aug. 14. |
| Tokyo, Japan | Typhoon kills 681; Sept. 21. |
| Honshu, Japan | Typhoon kills 679, many missing, extensive damage; Sept. 27–28. |
| Kanash, U.S.S.R. | Aeroflot TU-104 crashes, 65 dead; Oct. 17. |
| Chicago, Ill. | Fire in parochial school, 95 dead; Dec. 1. |
| Bogotá, Colombia | Department store fire, 84 dead; Dec. 16. |

## 1959

| | |
|---|---|
| Java | Train derails, 92 dead; May 28. |
| Fukien coast, China | Typhoon claims 2,334 lives; Aug. 20. |
| Honshu, Japan | Typhoon kills more than 4,400; Sept. 26–27. |
| Jalisco and Colima, Mexico | Hurricane causes mudslides and floods, 1,000 (?) dead; Oct. 27–28. |
| Fréjus, France | Flood caused by Malpasset Dam failure takes 412 lives; Dec. 2. |

## 1960

| | |
|---|---|
| Coalbrook, South Africa | Coal mine cave-in and explosion, over 400 dead; Jan. 21. |
| Zwickau, E. Germany | Mine explosion, 123 dead; Feb. 22. |
| Agadir, Morocco | Earthquakes and tidal waves destroy city, 20,000 (?) dead; Feb. 29–Mar. 1. |
| Near Tell City, Ind. | Northwest Electra explodes in flight, 63 dead; Mar. 17. |
| Chile, Japan and Hawaii | Earthquake series, volcanic eruptions, landslides and tsunami cause widespread devastation; in Chile over 2,000 dead and $550 million damage; in Hawaii 61 dead and $22 million damage; in Japan 138 dead and $50 million damage; May 22–29. |
| Guatemala City, Guatemala | Hospital fire, 225 dead; July 19. |
| Near Dakar, Senegal | Air France Constellation crashes into sea, 63 dead; Aug. 29. |
| Boston, Mass. | Eastern Airlines Electra crashes into harbor on takeoff, 62 dead; Oct. 4. |
| East Pakistan | Cyclones and tidal waves take 10,000 (?) lives; Oct. 10 and Oct. 31. |

| | |
|---|---|
| Amude, Syria | Movie house fire takes 152 lives; Nov. 13. |
| Pardubice, Czech. | Two trains collide, 110 dead; Nov. 14. |
| New York, N.Y. | United DC-8 and TWA Constellation collide, 134 dead; Dec. 16. |
| New York, N.Y. | Fire aboard unfinished aircraft carrier *Constellation* at Brooklyn Navy Yard, 50 dead, $58 million damage; Dec. 19. |

## 1961

| | |
|---|---|
| Berg, Belgium | Airplane crash of Sebena Boeing 707 takes 73 lives including 18 U.S. figure skaters; Feb. 15. |
| In the Persian Gulf | British ship *Dara* burns, over 200 dead; Apr. 8. |
| East Pakistan | Typhoon plus tidal wave kills 2,000 (?); May 9. |
| Off Mozambique | Portuguese *Save* burns and explodes, 227 dead; July 8. |
| Dolná, Suce, Czech. | Coal gas explosion kills 108; July 8. |
| Near Chicago, Ill. | TWA Constellation crashes, 78 dead; Sept. 1. |
| Shannon, Ireland | Charter DC-6 crashes, 83 dead; Sept. 10. |
| Japan | Typhoon kills 185; Sept. 16–17. |
| Near Calcutta, India | Express train derailed, over 500 dead; Oct. 20. |
| Belize, Brit. Honduras | Hurricane devastates city, causing 250 (?) deaths and $150 million damage; Oct. 31. |
| Near Richmond, Va. | Charter Constellation airliner crashes in woods, 77 dead; Nov. 8. |
| Southern Mexico | Hurricane takes 330 lives; Nov. 14. |
| Niteroi, Brazil | Circus fire, over 320 dead; Dec. 17. |
| Catanzaro, Italy | Train falls into gorge, 69 dead; Dec. 23. |

## 1962

| | |
|---|---|
| Woerden, Neth. | Two trains collide, 91 dead; Jan. 8. |
| Mt. Huscarán, Peru | Andean avalanche buries over 3,000; Jan. 10. |
| Voelklingen, W. Germany | Coal mine explosion, 298 dead; Feb. 7. |
| New York, N.Y. | American Boeing 707 plunges into Jamaica Bay, 95 dead; Mar. 1. |
| Near Douala, Cameroon | British DC-7 crashes in jungle, 111 dead; Mar. 4. |
| Western Pacific Ocean | Charter Constellation disappears, 107 lost; Mar. 16. |
| Tokyo, Japan | Three-train collision, 163 dead; May 3. |
| Paris, France | Air France Boeing 707 crashes, 130 dead; June 3. |
| Guadeloupe, West Indies | Air France Boeing 707 crashes, 113 dead; June 22. |

| | |
|---|---|
| Northwestern Iran | Earthquake kills over 10,000; Sept. 1. |
| Barcelona, Spain | Flash flood kills more than 470, damage $80 million; Sept. 27. |
| Thailand | Cyclone claims 769 lives and 142 missing, damage $19 million; Oct. 27. |
| Lima, Peru | Varig Boeing 707 crashes, 97 dead; Nov. 27. |
| Northern Europe | Winter-storm floods cause 309 deaths in Germany and takes lives in other countries; Dec. 31. |

## 1963

| | |
|---|---|
| Ankara, Turkey | Turkish Air Force plane and Lebanese Viscount collide, 95 dead; Feb. 1. |
| Bali, Indonesia | Volcanic eruption of Mt. Agung, 1,584 dead; Mar. 18. |
| In North Atlantic | Nuclear submarine *Thresher* sinks with 129 aboard in U.S. Navy's worst peacetime submarine disaster; Apr. 10. |
| East Pakistan | Storms and tidal waves in Bay of Bengal area take 22,000 (?) lives; May 28–29. |
| Off Southern Alaska | Northwest DC-7 charter crashes, 101 dead; June 3. |
| Skopje, Yugoslavia | Earthquake devastates city, 1,030 dead; July 26. |
| Zurich, Switzerland | Swissair Caravelle crashes, 80 dead; Sept. 4. |
| Near Salinas, Calif. | Farm bus and freight train collide, 32 dead; Sept. 17. |
| Caribbean area | Hurricane Flora kills 4,000 (?) in Haiti and Cuba; Oct. 1–9. |
| Near Belluno, Italy | Landslide near Vaiont Dam causes overflow, about 2,200 dead; Oct. 9. |
| Indianapolis, Ind. | Explosion and fire at Coliseum, 74 dead; Oct. 31. |
| Near Yokohama, Japan | Two passenger trains hit derailed freight train, 163 dead; Nov. 9. |
| Omuta, Japan | Coal mine explosion, 446 dead; Nov. 9. |
| Northern Haiti | Floods and landslides take 500 (?) lives; Nov. 14–15. |
| Near Norwalk, Conn. | Fire in nursing home for aged, 63 dead; Nov. 23. |
| Montreal, Canada | Trans-Canada DC-8 crashes, 118 dead; Nov. 29. |

## 1964

| | |
|---|---|
| Innsbruck, Austria | British airliner crashes, 83 dead; Feb. 29. |
| Minden, Nevada | Nonscheduled airliner crashes near Lake Tahoe, 85 dead; Mar. 1. |
| Alaska | Earthquake responsible for 114 deaths; Mar. 27. |
| Clark Field, Philippines | U.S. military transport crashes, 75 dead; May 11. |

|  |  |
|---|---|
| Lima, Peru | Riot at soccer game, 328 dead; May 24. |
| Near Oporto, Portugal | Train wreck kills 94; July 26. |
| Near Caracas, Venezuela | Bridge over Caroni Falls collapses, 50 (?) dead; Aug. 23. |
| Near Granada, Spain | African Transport DC-6 crashes, 80 dead; Oct. 2. |
| Southern Louisiana | Hurricane kills 36; Oct. 3. |

**1965**

|  |  |
|---|---|
| In the Andes, Chile | Chilean DC-6 crashes, 87 dead; Feb. 6. |
| Atlantic Ocean | Eastern DC-7 crashes near Kennedy Airport, 84 dead; Feb. 8. |
| Central Chile | Earthquake kills 400, damage $200 million; Mar. 28. |
| Midwest U.S. | Tornadoes kill 272; Apr. 11. |
| Barisal, East Pakistan | Cyclones and tidal waves kill 12,000 to 20,000, million homeless; May 11–12. |
| Cairo, Egypt | Pakistani Boeing 707 crashes, 119 dead; May 20. |
| Bihar State, India | Coal mine explosion, 400 (?) dead; May 28. |
| Kyushu, Japan | MIne accident kills 236; June 1. |
| Kakanj, Yugoslavia | Gas explosion claims 108; June 7. |
| Near El Toro, Calif. | Military plane hits mountain, 84 dead; June 25. |
| Near Searcy, Ark. | Explosion and fire at missile site, 53 dead; Aug. 9. |
| Southern U.S. and Bahamas | Hurricane Betsy claims 88 lives, $1.5 billion damage; Sept. 7–10. |
| Near Durban, South Africa | Train derailed, 81 dead; Oct. 4. |
| In the Caribbean | Panamanian cruise ship *Yarmouth Castle* sinks after fire, 89 dead; Nov. 13. |
| Karachi, Pakistan | Cyclone takes 10,000 (?) lives; Dec. 15. |

**1966**

|  |  |
|---|---|
| Rio de Janeiro | Deluge and landslides kill over 300; Jan. 11–13. |
| French Alps | Air India Boeing 707 crashes into Mt. Blanc, 117 dead; Jan. 24. |
| Chandpur Port, East Pakistan | Passenger launch and steamer collide, 80 dead; Jan. 30. |
| Tokyo, Japan | Japanese Boeing 727 plunges into Tokyo Bay, 133 dead; Feb. 4. |
| Honshu, Japan | BOAC Boeing 707 caught fire and crashed into Mt. Fujiyama, 124 dead; Mar. 5. |
| Lumding Junction, India | Train explosion kills 55; Apr. 20. |
| Near Ardmore, Okla. | Military charter plane crash, 83 dead; Apr. 22. |
| Eastern Turkey | Earthquake kills 2,529, renders 100,000 homeless; Aug. 19. |

|  |  |
|---|---|
| Belgrade, Yugoslavia | British airliner crashes on landing, 96 dead; Aug. 31. |
| Caribbean and Mexico | Hurricane Inez claims 300 (?): Sept. 25–Oct. 1. |
| Aberfan, Wales | Avalanche of coal slag kills 116 children and 28 adults; Oct. 21. |
| In the Gulf of Tonkin | U.S. aircraft carrier *Oriskany* catches fire, 43 dead; Oct. 26. |
| Kosi River, India | Indian vessel sinks, over 100 dead; Oct. 26. |
| Northern Italy | Flood waters of Po and Arno rivers kill 113, destroy priceless art treasures in Florence and elsewhere; Nov. 3–4. |
| Off Crete | Greek ferry *Heraklion* sinks, 217 dead; Dec. 8. |
| Bratislava, Czechoslovakia | Bulgarian airliner crashes, 82 dead; Nov. 24. |

**1967**

|  |  |
|---|---|
| Rio de Janeiro and São Paulo states, Brazil | Floods kill more than 600; Jan.-Mar. |
| Nicosia, Cyprus | Swiss airliner crashes, 126 dead; Apr. 20. |
| Brussells, Belgium | Department store fire, 322 dead; May 22. |
| French Pyrenees | British airliner crashes into Mont Canigou, 88 dead; June 3. |
| Langenweddingin, East Germany | Train collision with gasoline truck, 82 dead; June 6. |
| Near Hendersonville, N.C. | Piedmont Boeing 727 collides with private plane, 82 dead; July 19. |
| Off Vietnam | U.S. aircraft carrier *Forrestal* crippled by fire, 134 dead; July 25. |
| Venezuela | Earthquakes kill 277, damage in Caracas area $15 million; July 30–31. |
| Cincinnati, Ohio | TWA Convair crashes, 70 dead; Nov. 5. |
| Lisbon, Portugal | Floodwaters kill 457; Nov. 26. |
| Near Pt. Pleasant, W. Va. | Suspension bridge collapses into Ohio River at rush hour, 46 dead; Dec. 15. |

**1968**

|  |  |
|---|---|
| Eastern Mediterranean | Israeli submarine *Dakar* sinks, 69 dead; Jan. 26. |
| Western Mediterranean | French submarine *Minerve* sinks, 52 lost; Jan. 27. |
| Wellington Harbor, New Zealand | Ferry *Wahine* hits reef and sinks, 51 lost; Apr. 10. |
| Near Windhoek, South Africa | South African Boeing 707 crashes, 123 dead; Apr. 20. |
| Near Dawson, Texas | Braniff Electra crashes, 85 dead; May 3. |
| Midwest U.S. | Tornadoes hit 11 states, 71 dead; May 15. |
| Atlantic Ocean, off Azores | U.S. nuclear submarine *Scorpion* lost at sea with 99 aboard; May 27. |

| | |
|---|---|
| The Philippines | Earthquake claims over 300 lives in greater Manila area; Aug. 2. |
| Gujarat, India | Floods kill 1,000 (?); Aug. 8–14. |
| Northeastern Iran | Earthquake kills 12,000 (?); Aug. 31. |
| Off Nice, France | Air France Caravelle crashes, 95 dead; Sept. 11. |
| Farmington, W. Va. | Coal mine explosion and fire, 78 dead; Nov. 20. |

## 1969

| | |
|---|---|
| Southern Calif. | Floods take 95 lives; Jan. 25–29. |
| Northeast U.S. | Blizzard claims 64 lives; Feb. 9–10. |
| La Coruba, Venezuela | Venezuelan DC-9 crashes into suburb of Maracaibo, 154 dead; Mar. 16. |
| Barroterán, Mexico | Mine explosion and fires kill 180; Mar. 31. |
| Dacca, E. Pakistan | Cyclone kills 500 (?); Apr. 15. |
| South China Sea | U.S. destroyer *Evans* sliced in two by Australian carrier *Melbourne*, 74 lost. |
| Los Angeles de San Rafael, Spain | New restaurant collapses, 53 dead; June 15. |
| Jaipur, India | Passenger train rammed by freight train, 85 dead; July 15. |
| Gulf Coast and Eastern U.S. | Hurricane Camille claims 170 lives, thousands left homeless, floods in West Virginia take another 110 lives; total damage, $1.5 billion; Aug. 17–19. |

## 1970

| | |
|---|---|
| Near Buenos Aires, Argentina | Commuter train struck by express train, 236 dead; Feb. 4. |
| Val d'Isère, France | Avalanche kills 39 at youth hostel; Feb. 10. |
| In the Caribbean | Dominican DC-9 crashes in sea near Santo Domingo, 102 dead; Feb. 15. |
| Northern Nigeria | Train crash kills 150, crash of truck carrying survivors takes additional 52 lives, Feb. 16. |
| In the Mediterranean | French submarine *Eurydice* sinks, 57 dead; Mar. 4. |
| Kutahya, Turkey | Earthquake claims over 1,000; Mar. 28. |
| Osaka, Japan | Gas main explosions kill 73; Apr. 8. |
| Plateau d'Assy, France | Avalanche hits sanatorium killing 72, mostly children; Apr. 16. |
| Oradea, Rumania | Floods cause extensive damage and take 200 (?) lives; May 11–23. |
| Northern Peru | Earthquake claims 70–80,000 lives and injures 200,000; May 31. |
| Barcelona, Spain | British charter Comet jet crashes during landing, 112 dead; July 4. |
| Toronto, Canada | Air Canada DC-8 crashes, 108 dead; July 5. |
| New Delhi, India | Flash flood sweeps buses and other vehicles into gorge, 600 dead; July 22. |

| | |
|---|---|
| In Caribbean, off Nevis | Overcrowded ferry sinks, 125 (?) lost; Aug. 1. |
| Near Cuzco, Peru | Peruvian airliner crashes, 100 dead; Aug. 1. |
| Silver Plume, Colo. | Charter plane carrying Wichita State football team crashes into Rockies, 30 dead; Oct. 2. |
| Saint-Laurent-du-Pont, France | Fire in dance hall kills 146; Nov. 1. |
| East Pakistan | Storm wave ravages Ganges-Bramaputra river delta area, death toll estimated at 500,000 in worst disaster of century; Nov. 13. |
| Huntington, W. Va. | Southern Airways DC-9 crashes carrying Marshall Univ. Football team, 75 killed; Nov. 14. |

## 1971

| | |
|---|---|
| Moscow, U.S.S.R. | Aeroflot 11–18 crashes during takeoff, 90 dead; Jan. 1. |
| Southern California | Earthquake kills 64 in Los Angeles area, damage $1 billion; Feb. 9. |
| Lima, Peru | Avalanche kills 600 (?); Feb. 19. |
| Bingol, Turkey | Earthquake claims 800; May 23. |
| Wuppertal, W. Germany | Two trains collide, 47 schoolchildren dead; May 28. |
| Honshu, Japan | Japanese airliner collides with jet fighter plane, 162 dead; July 30. |
| Near Juneau, Alaska | Alaska Airlines Boeing 727 crashes into mountain, all 111 passengers killed; Sept. 4. |
| Orissa State, India | Cyclone and tidal wave claims 10,000 (?) lives in Bay of Bengal area; Oct. 29. |
| Seoul, S. Korea | Hotel fire kills 163; Dec. 25. |

## 1972

| | |
|---|---|
| Buffalo Creek, W. Va. | Flash flood from mine waste dam failure causes 118 deaths; Feb. 26. |
| United Arab Emirates | Danish charter plane crashes, 112 dead; Mar. 14. |
| Iraq | Mercury poisoning, over 100 dead; Mar.–Apr. |
| Iran | Earthquake kills over 5,000; Apr. 10. |
| Kellogg, Idaho | Fire in Sunshine Silver Mine; 91 miners dead; May 2. |
| Palermo, Italy | Alitalia DC-8 hits mountain, all 115 passengers killed; May 6. |
| Near Buenos Aires, Argentina | Liberian tanker *Tien Chee* and British freighter *Royal Grange* collide, 83 lost; May 11. |
| Osaka, Japan | Fire in nightclub on top of department store, 115 dead; May 13. |
| Northwest Rhodesia | Coal mine explosion, 427 dead; June 6. |
| Rapid City, S. Dak. | Flash flood kills 427, damage $120 million; June 10. |

| | |
|---|---|
| Eastern United States | Hurricane Agnes claims 134 lives, $1.7 billion damage; June 10–20. |
| Soissons, France | Train collision in tunnel caused by fallen rocks, 107 dead; June 17. |
| London, England | BEA jet airliner crash, 118 dead; June 18. |
| Luzon, Philippines | Typhoon and heavy rains cause landslides and flooding, 427 dead; July–Aug. |
| East Berlin, E. Germany | Charter East German airliner explodes and crashes in suburban area, 156 dead; Aug. 14. |
| Saltillo, Mexico | Passenger train derails, 204 dead; Oct. 6. |
| Krasnaya, U.S.S.R. | Ilyushin-18 crashes, 176 dead; Oct. 15. |
| Canary Islands | Spanish charter airliner crashes, 155 dead; Dec. 3. |
| Seoul, S. Korea | Theater fire takes 50 lives; Dec. 3. |
| Managua, Nicaragua | Earthquake levels city, 10,000 dead; Dec. 23. |
| Near Miami, Fla. | Eastern Airlines jetliner crashes into Everglades, 98 dead; Dec. 29. |

## 1973

| | |
|---|---|
| Kano, Nigeria | Egyptian Boeing 707 carrying Moslem pilgrims to Mecca crashes, 176 dead; Jan. 22. |
| Staten Island, N.Y. | Liquid gas tank explosion and fire, 40 workmen killed; Feb. 10. |
| Rangoon River, Burma | Collision between passenger ferry and Japanese freighter, about 200 dead; Feb. 22. |
| Bangladesh | Smallpox epidemic reported March 1, death rate 1,000 a month. |
| Basel, Switzerland | British charter carrying women on one-day shopping trip crashes, 104 dead; Apr. 10. |
| Dacca, Bangladesh | Two riverboats collide, 250 dead; May 5. |
| Indonesia | Series of spring storms take 1,650 lives; April. |
| Paris, France | Brazilian Boeing 707 crashes at Orly, 122 dead; July 11. |
| Boston, Mass. | Delta jetliner crashes in fog at Logan Airport, 88 dead; July 31. |
| Central Mexico | Earthquake, over 500 dead; Aug. 28. |
| Kumamoto, Japan | Department store fire, 101 dead; Nov. 29. |
| Off Ecuador | Passenger ferry capsizes, 142 dead; Dec. 24. |

## 1974

| | |
|---|---|
| Pago Pago, Samoa | Pan Am jet crashes, 92 dead; Jan. 31. |
| São Paulo, Brazil | Fire in 25-story bank building kills 188; Feb. 1. |
| Paris, France | Turkish DC-10 crashes on takeoff after cargo door failure in worst civil aviation disaster to date, 345 dead; Mar. 3. |
| Sahel region, W. Africa, Ethiopia | Drought and famine in sub-Sahara's report of Mar. 3 estimated a 1973 death toll of 100,000 persons in the Sahel; 50,000–100,000 death toll in Ethiopia. |
| Andes Mountains, Peru | Landslide takes 250 lives; Apr. 25. |
| Leningrad, U.S.S.R. | Soviet Ilyushin 18 crashes, 108 dead; Apr. 27. |
| Bali, Indonesia | Pan Am Boeing 707 crashes, 107 dead; Apr. 27. |
| Bangladesh coast | Motor launch capsizes, 250 dead; May 1. |
| Near Bogotá, Colombia | Landslide kills 200 (?); June 28. |
| Honduras | Hurricane Fifi claims about 8,000 lives; Sept. 18–19. |
| The Black Sea | Soviet destroyer burns, 200 (?) dead; Sept. 26. |
| Upperville, Va. | TWA Boeing 727 crashes, 92 dead; Dec. 1. |
| Columbia, Sri Lanka | Dutch DC-8 crashes, 191 dead; Dec. 4. |
| Northern Pakistan | Earthquake kills 5,200 (?); Dec. 28. |

## 1975

| | |
|---|---|
| Southern Thailand | Floods claim 130 lives; Jan. 10–11. |
| Near Dacca, Bangladesh | Passenger ferry sinks, 100 (?) dead; Jan. 25. |
| London, England | Subway train crash, 41 dead; Feb. 28. |
| Saigon, S. Vietnam | U.S. Air Force transport jet carrying orphans crashes on takeoff, 155 dead; Apr. 4. |
| New York, N.Y. | Eastern Boeing 727 crashes, 113 dead; Apr. 24. |
| Near Agadir, Morocco | Charter Boeing 707 crashes, 188 dead; Aug. 3. |
| Eastern Turkey | Earthquake claims 2,300 (?) lives; Sept. 6. |
| Bihar, India | Coal mine explosion and flooding, 700 (?) dead; Dec. 27. |

## 1976

| | |
|---|---|
| Saudi Arabia | Lebanese jetliner crashes in desert, 82 dead; Jan. 1. |
| Guatemala | Earthquake devastates much of country, death toll estimated 22,000, 1 million homeless; Feb. 4. |
| Trento, Italy | Cable car accident, 42 dead; Mar. 9. |
| Northeastern Italy | Earthquake claims up to 1,200 lives, extensive damage; May 6. |
| Tangshan, China | Earthquake leaves industrial city in ruins, death toll may reach over 100,000; July 28. |

## 1977

| | |
|---|---|
| Cape Cod, Mass. | Panamanian-registered tanker *Grand Zenith* sinks, 38 dead; Jan. 11. |
| Moscow, U.S.S.R. | Fire of undetermined origin ravages wing of Rossiya Hotel—one of world's largest, 45 dead; Feb. 25. |
| Bucharest, Rumania | Earthquake measuring 7.5 on the Richter scale strikes, killing 1,500 (?); Mar. 4. |
| Tenerife, Canary Islands | KLM 747 and Pan American 747 collide on runway at Tenerife Airport in worst air disaster on record, 581 die; Mar. 27. |
| Southeast Bangladesh | Typhoon-spawned floods and tidal waves kill 600; Apr. 1. |
| Southgate, Ky. | Nightclub fire, 164 dead; May 28. |
| Columbia, Tenn. | Jail fire, 42 die; June 26. |
| Johnstown, Penn. | Floods kill 68; July 19–20. |
| Westwego, La. | Grain elevator blows up, 35 dead; Dec. 22. |

## 1978

| | |
|---|---|
| Near Bombay, India | Air India 747 explodes and crashes into the sea, 213 dead; Jan. 1. |
| Orissa, India | Tornadoes kill 500 people; Apr. 16. |
| Northern India | Monsoon flooding kills 1,200 (?); June–Sept. |
| Tarragona, Spain | Tank truck carrying liquid industrial gas explodes, 183 dead; July 11. |
| Near San Diego, Calif. | Mid-air crash between a Boeing 727 and Cessna 172, 150 dead; Sept. 25. |

## 1979

| | |
|---|---|
| Texas and Oklahoma | Storm-spawned tornadoes leave 60 dead; Apr. 10. |
| Chicago, Ill. | American Airlines DC-10 crashes after takeoff, 275 dead—highest death toll in U.S. aviation history; May 25. |
| Morvi, India | Monsoon flooding and tidal waves kill as many as 15,000; Aug. 11. |
| Near Fastnet, England | Irish Sea squalls cause 23 boats competing in Fastnet race to overturn or be abandoned, 18 dead; Aug. 14. |
| Antarctica | New Zealand DC-10 crashes into mountain, 257 dead; Nov. 28. |

## 1980

| | |
|---|---|
| Near Spirit Lake, Wash. | Mount St. Helens erupts, 57 dead or missing; May 18. |
| Riyadh, Saudi Arabia | Tristar jet crashes and burns after an emergency landing at Riyadh Airport, 301 dead; Aug. 19. |
| Northern Algeria | Earthquake kills 4,500 (?); Oct. 10. |
| Ortuella, Spain | Explosion in a school kills 64; Oct. 23. |
| Las Vegas, Nev. | Fire sweeps through a wing of the new MGM Grand Hotel, 84 die; Nov. 21. |
| Naples, Italy | Earthquake and tremors leave thousands homeless, 4,800 dead; Nov. 23. |

| | |
|---|---|
| Harrison, N.Y. | Fire, believed caused by arsonist, damages Stauffer Inn, 26 dead; Dec. 4. |

## 1981

| | |
|---|---|
| Dublin, Ireland | Discotheque fire kills 44; Feb. 14. |
| Mainland China | Sichuan and Hubei provinces flooding kills 1,300 (?); July. |
| Kansas City, Mo. | Hyatt Regency Hotel skywalks collapse, 114 dead, hundreds injured; July 17. |
| Corsica | Yugoslav DC-9 crashes into mountain, 174 dead; Dec. 1. |

## 1982

| | |
|---|---|
| Washington, D.C. | Air Florida 737 crashes into the Potomac River after takeoff, 78 dead; Jan. 13. |
| Kenner, La. | Pan American 727 crashes after takeoff, 153 dead, including 8 on the ground; July 9. |
| Los Angeles, Calif. | Apartment house fire kills 24; Sept. 4. |
| El Salvador and Guatemala | Floods and landslides kill over 1,300; Sept. 17–21. |
| Afghanistan | Gas truck explosion in Salang Tunnel—guerrillas take credit, 1,000–3,000 dead; Nov. 2. |
| Biloxi, Miss. | County jail fire kills 29; Nov. 8. |

## 1983

| | |
|---|---|
| Turin, Italy | Movie theater fire kills 64; Feb. 13. |
| India | Monsoon rains and flooding kill 900; June. |
| Near Madrid, Spain | Columbia Boeing 747 crashes, 183 dead; Nov. 27. |
| Eastern Turkey | Earthquake kills 1,300 (?); Oct. 30. |
| Madrid, Spain | Discotheque fire kills 83, most of whom are teenagers; Dec. 17. |

## 1984

| | |
|---|---|
| Africa | Persistent drought, particularly in Sahel and East Africa, created famine that already has claimed tens of thousands of lives. |
| Near Tokyo, Japan | Fire in an undersea coal mine kills 83 miners; Jan. 18. |
| Near Cubatao, Brazil | Oil line explosion and fires kill over 500; Feb. 25. |
| Feira de Santana, Brazil | Viral disease kills 252 children; May 13. |
| Near Luanda, Angola | Train wreck kills 50 (?); June 18. |
| Malaysia | Ferry capsizes off the State of Sabah, nearly 200 drown; Aug. 13. |
| Mexico City, Mexico | Liquid petroleum gas tank explodes, thousands homeless, nearly 500 dead; Nov. 19. |
| Bhopal, India | Toxic gas leak at Union Carbide chemical plant, over 2,000 dead, tens of thousands injured; Dec. 3. |

# INDEX

## A

Aberfan, Wales, slag heap disaster, 148–153
Agadez, Niger, 176
airplane disasters, 83–87, 132–141
*Andrea Doria*, luxury liner, 125–131
Asch Building, New York City, 25, 28
avalanches, 160–165

## B

Babylon express, train, 110–117
Baltz, Steven, 135
Belaunde Terry, Fernando, 146
Biloxi, Mississippi, hurricane, 157, 158
"Bomba," 145
Bureau of Mines, 23

## C

Callejón de Huaylas, 166–171
Camille, hurricane, 154–159
Chad, famine, 175
Chimaltenango, Guatemala, earthquake, 186
coal mine disasters, 16–23
coal mine safety regulations, 23
Crefisul Investment Bank, São Paulo, Brazil, fire, 178–
    183
Cocoanut Grove Club, fire, 66–73

## D

"Death Valley Railroad," 115

## E

earthquakes, 166–171, 184–189
*Eastland*, steamer, 30–37
Elizabeth II, 153
Empire State Building, 82–87
Ethiopia, famine, 175, 176
explosions (*see also* coal mine disasters), 48–55, 96–103,
    190–195

## F

Fairmont Coal Company, 18
famines, 172–177
fires (*see also* explosions), 24–29, 66–73, 74–81, 88–95,
    178–183
fire safety regulations, 28, 71, 94, 183

## G

Gale, Rich, 208
*Grandcamp*, freighter, 96–103
Guatemala City, earthquake, 184–189

## H

Hartford, Connecticut, circus fire, 74–81
*Hindenburg*, dirigible, 56–65
Hitler, Adolf, 55, 58
Huacos, legend of the, 120, 122
Huaraz, Peru, earthquake, 169
Huascarán, mountain, Peru, 168
Huaylas Valley, *see* Callejón de Huaylas
hurricanes, 154–159
Hyatt Regency Hotel, Kansas City, 206–211

## I

*Ile de France*, luxury liner, 129, 130
Independent School, New London, Texas, 48–55

## J

Jones, Charles (Buck), 68
Juan Comalapa, Guatemala, earthquake, 187

## K

Kansas City, Missouri, hotel disaster, 206–211

## L

LaGuardia, Fiorello, 86
landslides, *see* avalanches
Le Dôme, mountain, 162, 164
Lehmann, Ernst, 58, 59
Lima, Peru, soccer riot, 142–147
"Little Miss 1565," 77, 80
Long Island Rail Road, 112, 114, 115

## M

Mali, famine, 175
Mauritania, famine, 175
Merthyr Vale mine, 152, 153
Monongah, West Virginia, coal mine disaster, 16–23
*Morro Castle*, passenger ship, 38–47
Mount St. Helens, volcano eruption, 196–205

## N

National Coal Board (British), 153
National Stadium, Lima, Peru, 142–147
New London, Texas, school explosion, 48–55
Niger, famine, 175
Nixon, Pat, 169
*Noronic*, pleasure ship, 104–109

## P

Park Slope, Brooklyn, plane crash, 132–141
Pascagoula, Alabama, hurricane, 157
Pass Christian, Mississippi, hurricane, 155, 157, 158
Patzicía, Guatemala, earthquake, 186–187
Pazos, Angel Eduardo, 144, 145, 146
Peachtree Hotel, *see* Winecoff Hotel
Pentglas Junior and Infants School, Aberfan, Wales, 148–153
Peru, earthquake of 1970, 166–171
plane crashes, *see* airplane disasters
Plateau d'Assy, France, 164
Prince Philip, 153

## R

Ranrahirca, Peru, earthquake, 166–171
Red Cross, 55, 158
Ringling Bros. and Barnum & Bailey Circus, 77
Roman, Ruth, 126, 129
Roosevelt, Franklin, D., 55

## S

Sahara Desert, famine, 175, 176
*Sahel*, Africa, famine, 175, 176
St. Barbara's Memorial Nursing Home, 23
Salvation Army, 158
São Paulo, Brazil, fire, 178–183
school disasters, 48–55, 148–153
Senegal, famine, 175
ship disasters, 30–37, 38–47, 104–109, 124–131
Smith, William F., 85
soccer riot, Lima, Peru, 142–147

Staten Island, New York, plane crash, 144–148
Steve Miller Band, 208
*Stockholm*, motorship, 124–131

## T

Tarragona, Spain, tanker explosion, 190–195
Tauregs, 176
Texas City, Texas, explosion, 96–103
Timbuktu, Mali, 176
tornadoes, 154–159
Toutle, Washington, 196–205
train wrecks, 110–117
Triangle Shirtwaist Company, 24–29
twisters, *see* tornadoes

## U

UNICEF, and Sahara famine, 177
United Airlines, plane crash, 132–141
Upper Volta, famine, 175

## V

Val d'Isère, France, avalanche, 160–165
volcano, *see* Mount St. Helens

## W

Waco, Texas, tornado, 118–123
Waldheim, Kurt, 177
Waveland, Mississippi, hurricane, 157
Welansky, Barney, 71
*Wilmette*, see *Eastland*
Wilmott, Robert, 40, 47
Wilson, Harold, 153
Winecoff, W. F., 90, 92
Winecoff Hotel, Atlanta, 88–95

## Y

Yungay, Peru, earthquake, 166–171

## Z

Zumpango, Guatemala, earthquake, 187